The
Black Dot
Philosophy

A Strategic Roadmap for Conquering
Life's Toughest Challenges!

JERRY MARK FISH

Published by The Black Dot Philosophy, Inc.
Learn more at www.theblackdotphilosophy.com

ISBN 979-8-9904759-0-8 (paperback)
ISBN 979-8-9904759-1-5 (ebook)
ISBN 979-8-9904759-3-9 (hardcover)
ISBN 979-8-9904759-2-2 (audiobook)

Book Design: Clarity Designworks

Printed in the United States of America

This book is dedicated to my son, Tyler, whose love and wisdom have been my greatest sources of strength and inspiration. Your courage and insight have shaped me in ways you may never fully understand.

And in memory of the remarkable women who have shaped my life but are no longer with us:

To my mother, Judith Fish, whose strength and wisdom taught me so much in the little time we had together. She bravely fought a Stage 4 Breast Cancer diagnosis but lost the battle at the very young age of 41.

To my sister, Terri, who was a wonderful mother to her four children and a supportive wife to her husband Joe. Taken from us far too soon at age 30, she may be gone but is certainly not forgotten.

To my cousin, Debbie, who left us at age 36 from cancer. She was more of a sister than a cousin, and we were inseparable from the time we were little kids until she passed away. One of the most selfless people I've ever known, Debbie fought her illness to the very end. Her two young children and her husband, David, were her world and her inspiration to keep living.

To my Aunt Helen, who stepped in to help me and my siblings after my mother passed away. Her life was also tragically shortened due to an unexpected medical issue.

These amazing women played a huge role in my life, and I think about them every day.

WHY I FELT MOVED
TO WRITE THIS BOOK

Thank you for the opportunity to share my personal motivation behind writing *The Black Dot Philosophy*. The inspiration for this book stemmed from the complex, challenging, and uncertain times we are living in, both in the United States and globally.

The past few years, marked by the pandemic, conflicts, and significant social and political upheavals, have presented unprecedented challenges. These global events have affected individuals deeply, creating a sense of uncertainty and vulnerability. Witnessing the widespread impact of these events, I felt a strong need to contribute something that could help people navigate through these turbulent times.

The collective anxiety and stress brought on by these events are palpable. There's a growing need for ways to cope with the emotional toll they take. I want to provide a framework for you that not only addresses the external challenges but also the internal, emotional struggles that come with them.

The increasing polarization, not just in the United States but around the world, has created divisions within communities and families. Through this book, I aim to offer a perspective that transcends these divides, encouraging a focus on personal growth and understanding, which can be a unifying force.

The uncertain times have intensified personal challenges. People are reevaluating their lives, careers, and relationships. The *Black Dot*

Philosophy is meant to provide tools for individuals to transform these challenges into opportunities for growth and personal fulfillment.

I believe that when individuals are empowered to overcome their personal challenges, the effects extend beyond them. They can positively influence their families, communities, and, ultimately, society at large. By equipping individuals with the mindset and tools to navigate their struggles, the book aims to inspire a collective movement towards resilience, empathy, and positive change.

The Philosophy is also a culmination of my own experiences in facing and overcoming challenges. It's deeply personal, reflecting lessons I've learned and insights I've gained. I wanted to share this journey, hoping that the insights and strategies that helped me could resonate with and assist others.

The Black Dot Philosophy was born out of a desire to provide a beacon of hope, a guide for personal resilience and growth, in a time when the world is grappling with uncertainty and change. My hope is that this book serves as a resource for you to find strength within yourself, to transform your challenges into stepping stones for a more fulfilled and purposeful life.

CONTENTS

Foreword ix
Introduction. xi
The Journey Behind The Black Dot Philosophy xiii

STEP 1: UNCOVER YOUR CHALLENGES 1
Why you should identify your Black Dots 3
We can change how we think about problems 15
Use this guide to identify your Black Dots 19
Map your Black Dots. 21
Think about your own Black Dot journey 36

STEP 2: CHART YOUR COURSE 37
Purpose, Discipline, and Goals. 40
The Power of Purpose. 42
The Role of Discipline 65
The Importance of Goals 87
Think about your own Black Dot journey 114

STEP 3: COMMIT TO YOUR ASPIRATIONS. 115
The Art of Declarations 119
Face the fear of making a public Declaration 123
Embrace the Declaration Process 125
The Ripple Effect of Declarations. 128
How to create precise Declarations. 138
Deepen your emotional investment 144
Think about your own Black Dot journey 148

STEP 4: CRAFT YOUR GAME PLAN 149
   Use Strategy and Tactics to achieve your goals 155
   Understand Tactics so you can implement Strategies 163
   Craft strategies and tactics to tackle your Black Dots 174
   Create an Action Plan. 180
   Think about your own Black Dot journey 183

STEP 5: MAINTAIN YOUR MOMENTUM 185
   Accountability and personal responsibility 190
   Nurturing Commitment Over Time 195
   Adaptability 200
   Supportive Environments. 205
   The Power of Small Wins 209
   Think about your own Black Dot journey 211

STEP 6: HARVEST YOUR SUCCESS 213
   Recap of the Black Dot Philosophy 213
   Embrace your Black Dot journey 225
   What the collective impact looks like 227
   The never-ending journey:
      Black Dots as a lifelong endeavor 229
   Think about your own Black Dot journey 231
   Some Final Thoughts... 232

   Follow Up Questions 235
   The Black Dot Resource Library. 237
   Gratitude 249
   About the Author. 251

FOREWORD

In the canvas of life, we often find ourselves preoccupied with the multitude of colors that paint our existence. These colors represent our everyday experiences, joys, and sorrows. But amid this vibrant tapestry, there exist moments of contrast—moments that stand out, not because of their color, but because of their absence.

Imagine for a moment a white canvas with a single, solitary black dot. This black dot, though small, commands our attention. It represents the challenges, the obstacles, and the goals that define our journey. We call them our "Black Dots."

The Black Dot Philosophy is a profound perspective that invites us to recognize the significance of these Black Dots in our lives. It challenges us to declare our intentions, set audacious goals, and harness the power of discipline to achieve them. It encourages us to see adversity not as a roadblock but as an opportunity for growth. And it inspires us to make an impact that extends far beyond our own journey.

In this book, we will embark on a transformative journey together so that you can conquer your own Black Dots. I will walk you through the Black Dot Philosophy and, step-by-step, will unveil new layers to enhance your understanding. I will provide you with the tools, insights, and inspiration to turn your challenges into opportunities, your dreams into reality, and your life into a masterpiece.

Join us as we explore the power of the Black Dot Philosophy and discover that, amid the vast canvas of life, it's often the black dots that lead us to our most extraordinary colors.

INTRODUCTION

In the tapestry of our lives, we are confronted with a myriad of challenges and aspirations. Some are small, like the everyday inconveniences that pepper our routines, while others loom large, casting shadows of doubt and uncertainty. These challenges and goals, varying in size and significance, are the Black Dots that punctuate our existence.

Imagine, for a moment, if you could visualize these Black Dots, if you could see them scattered across the canvas of your life. Each one represents a challenge to overcome, a goal to achieve, a milestone to reach. This visualization, this clarity about your Black Dots, can be a transformative lens through which to view your journey.

Why are Black Dots significant? Because they hold the power to shape your path, to influence your choices, and to propel you toward a life of purpose and fulfillment. When you gain clarity about your Black Dots, you can prioritize them, strategize around them, and set your course with unwavering determination.

Think of it as a roadmap for your life. Just as a traveler navigates through a maze of roads and signs, you can navigate through the maze of your own challenges and goals. But to do so effectively, you must set priorities. You must determine which Black Dots deserve your attention, your energy, and your focus.

In the following pages, we will delve into the art of prioritization. We will explore how to categorize and organize your Black Dots based on their significance, ensuring that you tackle the most critical ones first. We will provide you with practical strategies for managing your challenges and aspirations with purpose and precision.

So, as we venture forward into the heart of the Black Dot Philosophy, remember that your Black Dots are not mere obstacles; they are opportunities. Opportunities for growth, for resilience, and for meaningful achievement. It is through the lens of your Black Dots that you will embark on a transformative journey, one that holds the promise of a life filled with purpose and possibility.

THE JOURNEY BEHIND
THE BLACK DOT PHILOSOPHY

I believe it's essential to explain the origins of the Black Dot Philosophy to give you an understanding of how it developed over the past thirty years from a simple conversation into a meaningful process for helping people conquer life's toughest challenges.

Like everyone else, I've faced personal challenges throughout my life. I want to acknowledge that, as tough as my challenges were and are today, they pale in comparison to the daunting challenges many people have historically faced and continue to face today. The pandemic has particularly highlighted this, revealing struggles among family members, friends, colleagues, and neighbors. Nobody is immune to life's challenges, though some face more significant hardships than others. Nonetheless, we all experience suffering and pain in our lives.

Think about it! How did notable individuals not only face incredible adversity but also persevere? Before the advent of personal development tools like the Black Dot Philosophy, people overcame challenges through sheer resilience and purpose.

However, this often came at a significant cost, including stress, anxiety, and emotional turmoil. A proven process like the Black Dot Philosophy could have alleviated some of the suffering associated with these struggles by providing a structured approach to managing challenges. The resilience of the human spirit continues to astound me.

Examples of Overcoming Adversity and Achieving Remarkable Goals

1. **Jackie Robinson,** who broke the color barrier in Major League Baseball and faced immense racial discrimination with courage and dignity.
2. **Viktor Frankl,** who survived the horrors of the Holocaust and went on to develop logotherapy, helping countless individuals find meaning in their lives.
3. **Abraham Lincoln,** who rose from humble beginnings to become one of the greatest presidents of the United States, leading the country through its Civil War and working to end slavery.
4. **Helen Keller,** who overcame the challenges of being deaf and blind to become a renowned author, activist, and lecturer, inspiring millions with her story.
5. **Louis Zamperini,** an Olympic athlete and World War II hero who survived a plane crash, weeks adrift at sea, and brutal treatment as a POW, later dedicating his life to helping others.

Before integrating the Black Dot Philosophy into my life, I attributed my ability to overcome challenges and achieve success to sheer tenacity driven by "purpose." Without purpose, my life story and professional success would likely have been very different, and not in a good way. However, without a system or process, life's challenges took a toll on me mentally and physically. I often found myself beaten down, even though I kept getting back up. Do you know the feeling?

The Black Dot Story

Early in my career with New York Life, I found myself struggling as a newly recruited but experienced manager. Seeking advice and guidance, I reached out to my mentor and Managing Partner of my office, Mike Kroplin. Mike suggested that we meet outside the office and have a conversation over lunch at his club, which overlooked the city and bay of San Francisco. He knew that the inspiring setting and the privacy of a small private room would be beneficial.

During our meeting, we addressed four areas where I needed to improve to meet my objectives. As the waiter was taking our order, Mike grabbed a napkin and drew four circles of varying sizes on it with a black pen. He then labeled each circle to represent the four improvement opportunities we had identified. The larger circles symbolized more significant challenges.

This simple yet powerful visual representation struck a chord with me. It provided a clear and structured way to address my challenges. Once we agreed on what each circle represented, we developed a game plan for each one. The idea was to reduce or ideally eliminate each circle. This approach proved to be highly effective, and within a year, I had addressed and eliminated all four challenges.

The concept of using circles to represent challenges evolved in my mind. I found the term "Black Dot" more symbolic and impactful than "Black Circles." The Black Dot Philosophy was born from this realization. It became a powerful tool that I integrated into my daily life to tackle virtually any challenge or goal, regardless of its severity or size.

That said, it wasn't until I decided to write this book that the word " philosophy" was added to the name Black Dot. I was asked to describe the process or system of the Black Dot in one word and after spending a good deal of time thinking about it, I came up with the word " philosophy". I had always just referred to it as the Black

Dot but when I really put some thought into it, I realized that it was more of a philosophy than anything else. The words system and process really describe the strategic aspect of The Black Dot which you will implement and then you "live" the philosophy of the Black Dot.

My childhood in a small suburb outside Cleveland, Ohio, was relatively uneventful and typical for a young boy. My parents, immigrants from Leeds, England, met and married in Cleveland before our family moved to the San Fernando Valley in Southern California. Here, I grew up alongside my siblings.

At age 15, I decided to try out for a local full-contact Football Team. With no experience in tackle football, I lacked technique and was eventually cut from the team. This was a humiliating experience, but it taught me the importance of determination and purpose. With encouragement from my mother, I tried out for another team and not only did I make the team, I became a starter by the first game of the season. I found a new passion for the game, and it would ultimately have a huge impact on me and forever change my life!

High School football brought new challenges. Like me, the other players from the team that had cut me had to try out for the high school team too! We were all treated exactly the same and no one was guaranteed anything from the coaches.

This was my opportunity to showcase what they missed out on when I got cut from their team just a year earlier. My hard work paid off as I became a starter and earned several accolades over the next three years including a first-team All-League selection and I was voted the "Most Inspirational Award" by my teammates, many who played on the team that had cut me. This experience instilled in me a confidence and competitive spirit that would serve me well in both my personal and professional life.

Another significant Black Dot emerged during my senior year of high school when my mother was diagnosed with Stage 4 breast cancer.

The news was devastating, and I struggled to cope with her illness and eventual passing. This period was marked by emotional turmoil and unhealthy coping mechanisms, highlighting the need for a structured process to handle life's challenges.

Those Black Dots in my youth were just the beginning of a life full of Black Dots. Several years after I finished college, I started an Estate and Financial Planning company, only to face betrayal from a business partner, leading to bankruptcy. Around the same time, my sister passed away from AIDS, leaving behind four young children. Despite these hardships, I joined New York Life in 1993. As you now know, my mentor used black circles to emphasize the significance of four improvement opportunities. In the following year, I began developing it into a more meaningful tool, which helped me achieve my professional goals despite battling depression and anxiety.

I was not only struggling with my career, but my marriage was coming to an end, and my cousin, who was like a sister to me, passed away from cancer that summer.

Thankfully, by then I had developed the Black Dot concept into an effective way to manage and resolve or eliminate personal challenges. Although it was in its infancy phase, it was instrumental in helping me get through the most challenging time of my life up to that point in time.

These Black Dots and many others shaped the development of the Black Dot Philosophy. By incorporating strategies and tactics to overcome personal and professional challenges, I created a system that has helped me and many others achieve success and resilience. The profound impact of the Black Dot Philosophy on my life during the 90s has only grown over the past two decades, proving to be an invaluable tool for overcoming significant challenges and achieving success both personally and professionally.

Throughout this book, I will share more about these Black Dots and how the Black Dot process played a crucial role in overcoming them. This philosophy is not just about professional success but also about personal growth and resilience.

STEP 1

UNCOVER YOUR CHALLENGES

As you now know, I have had my share of Black Dots varying in size, going back to my teenage years.

It wasn't until I formalized the Black Dot process for my sales and management team that I started to identify my Black Dots both personally and professionally.

That decision would later serve me well. Even though we had a successful joint custody arrangement with our son, my ex-wife notified me that she had met someone and they were going to get married. However, he lived in Ontario, Canada, and she was going to petition the Family Court to take our son with her, which obviously meant I would only get to see my son during the summer and some holidays.

It was a shock, to say the least, and I was determined to fight to keep him in the U.S. and gain custody as well. The Family Court ordered an evaluation by a trained professional to see what was best for my son. When the evaluations were complete, my attorney called to tell me the evaluator agreed that it was in my son's best interest to stay in California with me. She went on to say that it probably meant the judge would most likely side with me as well. Needless to say, I was incredibly hopeful.

Within a few weeks, after all negotiations failed, we were in court to start the trial. I was extremely optimistic—until the judge, in his opening comments, said, "In my day, the mother always took care of the children" My attorney and I were speechless, and my heart sank. My attorney leaned over and said that this particular judge was known to be "old school," and that even with the favorable evaluation, chances were slim that I would win. She then said that we should start to negotiate for the best possible custody arrangement in light of the judge's inappropriate comment. We weren't conceding, so the next court date was scheduled.

Emotionally, I was really struggling with the way this judge nonchalantly discarded my favorable evaluation and the fact that my son would be living in another country. It was The Black Dot Philosophy that allowed me to not only stay focused while my emotions were high but to develop strategies and tactics with my attorney's help to negotiate the best possible arrangement.

I was able to keep my emotions in check while coming up with a game plan to negotiate the best possible scenario that would allow me to see my son as often as humanly possible despite the fact that he would be moving over 3,000 miles away.

I know for a fact that without the Black Dot and the ancillary tools I used to implement the strategies and tactics we incorporated into our overall game plan, I would have let my emotions get the best of me and I would have said or done something I surely would come to regret. I was methodical about the strategies and tactics, which in the end allowed me to negotiate the best possible scenario for me and my son. It turns out that I was able to see him for every American and Canadian holiday and every summer too. In the end, it was the Black Dot Philosophy that helped me negotiate the best possible scenario for both me and my son! That said, when he was about to turn 14, another significant Black Dot emerged that would change everything which I will share with you later in the book.

Anyways, it was from that experience that I incorporated the Black Dot Philosophy into my daily life and used it for virtually any challenge or goal I had, regardless of the severity or size of the Black Dot. I also knew that I had to teach it to everyone I could from that point forward. As a side note, I'm a big believer in the act of forgiveness. When I think about it even today, I still get a little angry that this even happened but my former wife and I have a pretty good relationship now.

Why you should identify your Black Dots

The black dot symbol holds significant meaning in the Black Dot Philosophy. It serves as a metaphorical representation of the challenges, obstacles, or goals in a person's life. Each black dot symbolizes an area that demands attention or action for an individual to overcome or achieve something.

Here, in Step One, I am going to help you to think hard about the concept of Black Dots. We are going to look at "Why" you would want to identify your Black Dots. I'll show you what Black Dots look like in other peoples' lives.

Then, I will show you how to identify your challenges, the obstacles or problems in your life, and the issues or areas that require attention and action as "Black Dots."

The concept of the Black Dot

The Black Dot is a simple yet powerful tool that helps you to visually map out and confront life's challenges.

We use symbols as shorthand to express multiple concepts and complex ideas and to act as a reminder to take action.

This simple symbol, the Black Dot, ● represents six big ideas:

Idea One: A focus on specific challenges

⬤ is a visual tool to focus your attention on a particular issue in your life that requires improvement or growth. By identifying these "dots," you can clearly see the challenges you face in tackling them.

Idea Two: Awareness and Acknowledgment

⬤ encourages you to become aware of and acknowledge these challenges. When you recognize and visualize obstacles as black dots, you have taken the first step towards addressing them effectively.

Idea Three: Clarity and Prioritization

⬤ helps you prioritize challenges and set goals to tackle them. It's unlikely you only have one black dot in your life. Once you have identified a few, you will find that some dots are larger or more pressing than others, symbolizing their greater significance or urgency in your life.

Idea Four: Motivation for Action

⬤ is a constant reminder to take proactive steps in confronting the challenge, so it serves as a motivational symbol to encourage you to engage with, and overcome, the obstacles you face.

Idea Five: Empowerment

⬤ transforms an abstract, complex problem into concrete, tangible elements so that you can address the problem methodically. As a result, you will feel more empowered to tackle your Black Dots.

Idea Six: Symbol of Triumph

⬤ Overcoming each Black Dot becomes a symbol of triumph, representing your personal growth and the achievement of your goals in pursuit of a better and more fulfilling life.

Visualizing your Black Dots brings clarity

Visualizing your Black Dots is a key aspect of the Black Dot Philosophy. When we are vaguely aware of impending challenges or desirous of achieving something but haven't given it enough thought to make it concrete, we are in a state of confusion. If we are confused about what we should do, we tend not to take action, or take the wrong action. We may even put ourselves in danger of suffering overwhelm.

Visualizing our goals and challenges as Black Dots significantly aids us in prioritizing and strategizing how to deal with them. When you visualize your challenges and goals as Black Dots, they become more tangible and manageable.

A visual representation of your Black Dots on a piece of paper laid in front of you allows you to see your problems or objectives outside of yourself.

You get a clearer and more objective perspective so it's easier to prioritize them based on size, significance, urgency, or your own personal values.

You can quickly identify which dots are the largest or most impactful and therefore need immediate attention, and which ones can be addressed later.

You can determine what resources and actions are needed for each and develop a structured plan accordingly.

So, visualizing Black Dots enables you to devise a specific strategy for each challenge or goal. As you take action on your strategies, you can visually track your progress. Your Black Dots will change in size, symbolizing your progress. Some will resolve and disappear, or new dots may appear, indicating emerging challenges, or goals.

Seeing your Black Dots diminish in size or number is a powerful motivator. You have visual proof of your progress and success, and that encourages you, in turn, to take further action. The picture fuels persistence.

And if you, like most people, are facing multiple challenges, or pursuing several goals at once, visualizing them as Black Dots can bring clarity to complex situations because you can see at a glance what lies ahead and how your different challenges may be interconnected and influence one another.

The Black Dot Philosophy is a tool that helps you in both your personal and your professional life. It offers a holistic overview of the challenges and goals that face you in the entirety of your life, fostering a balanced approach to personal and professional development, and preventing you from looking at your situation with tunnel vision. It encourages you to take a comprehensive view of what lies ahead.

Visualizing black dots helps you to break down the abstract, and often overwhelming, concepts of challenges and goals into clear, manageable units. It aids in strategic planning, prioritization, and tracking progress. That makes it a practical and effective tool in the Black Dot Philosophy.

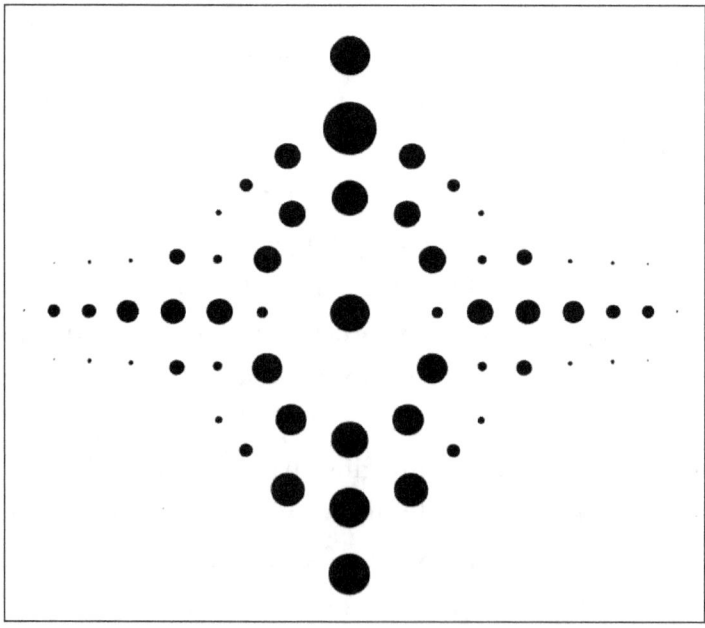

THE BLACK DOT VISUAL

How to read the Black Dot Visual

This visual represents the varying challenges and goals in our lives, depicted as black dots of different sizes. Each dot symbolizes a specific challenge or goal, the size indicating its significance or difficulty.

Examples of Challenges

It will be helpful to give you examples of what sort of challenges, or goals, you might class as smaller, or larger. Read through this list to get a conceptual understanding of the visual. Do you see how the "Black Dots" can represent various aspects of one's life journey?

1. Small Dot: Daily Routine—minor everyday tasks or habits
2. Slightly Larger Dot: Time Management—balancing work and personal life
3. Moderate Dot: Learning a New Skill—such as a language or instrument
4. Bigger Dot: Building Healthy Relationships—fostering meaningful connections
5. Larger Dot: Career Advancement—achieving professional growth
6. Significantly Large Dot: Financial Stability—managing and growing personal finances
7. Even Larger Dot: Personal Health—maintaining physical and mental well-being
8. Large Dot: Life Balance—finding equilibrium in all life aspects
9. Very Large Dot: Personal Legacy—what you wish to be remembered for
10. Largest Dot: Life Purpose—discovering and fulfilling your ultimate goal.

Keep this list in mind as you identify your own Black Dots. Use it to give you insight into how each dot can symbolize aspects of your own life's challenges and aspirations.

Let's break down how this visualization process works.

Clarity and awareness

When you visualize challenges or goals as black dots, it brings a level of clarity and awareness. Each dot represents a specific issue or objective. This visualization helps in acknowledging the existence of these challenges or goals, making them more tangible and less abstract.

Prioritization

Not all black dots are of equal size or significance. Some represent larger, more complex challenges or goals, while others might be smaller and less significant. By visualizing these dots, you can assess which ones you need to address at once and which you can deal with later. This prioritization is crucial for effective time management and resource allocation.

Strategizing

Once you've prioritized your Black Dots, you can start strategizing on how to tackle them. For larger dots, you might need a more comprehensive, long-term strategy, while smaller dots might be resolved with simpler, short-term actions. Visualizing these dots allows you to map out a clear strategy for each, considering the resources, time, and effort required.

Measuring progress

As you start addressing each Black Dot, you can visualize your progress. Dots that are being addressed might change in size or color in your visualization, indicating progress or resolution. This provides a sense of accomplishment and motivates you to continue working towards resolving other dots.

Adaptability

The visualization process is not static. As you progress in your journey, new black dots may appear, or existing ones might change in size or nature. Visualizing these changes allows you to adapt your strategies and actions accordingly, ensuring that you remain flexible and responsive to new challenges and opportunities.

Emotional and mental management

Visualizing your Black Dots can also be a way to manage emotional and mental load. By externalizing challenges and goals in this manner, you can prevent feelings of being overwhelmed. It provides a structured way to deal with issues, reducing stress and anxiety.

SUMMARY

Visualizing black dots as a part of the Black Dot Philosophy helps you to bring clarity to your challenges. It enables you to prioritize your action, measure your progress, and ensure adaptability, and it helps you to manage your emotional and mental load. This allows you to approach your challenges and goals in a more organized, strategic, and effective manner.

Why it's important to acknowledge the existence of your Black Dots

Once you acknowledge the existence of black dots in your life, you have taken a fundamental step in the Black Dot Philosophy. The consequences are profound.

You have recognized there are challenges to be addressed. Without recognizing these challenges, it's impossible to address them effectively. The first step in addressing any problem is to recognize that it exists.

Awareness leads to Action, so that acknowledging your Black Dots means you are accepting the presence of challenges, obstacles, or goals that require attention in your life.

Once you have recognized they exist, you're moving towards change or improvement. You have shifted from Denial to Action.

You may find you have been in denial about some of your problems or challenges. Perhaps, before you began to acknowledge them, you had only a hazy idea of what they were.

Acknowledging black dots represents a shift from a state of denial or avoidance to a state of action and responsibility. You are embracing reality: accepting reality as it is, not as you wish it to be.

When you define your Black Dots, you are admitting that certain areas of your life need work and can't be ignored.

You have increased your self-awareness and are becoming more honest with yourself. When you acknowledge your Black Dots, you take ownership of your challenges. This is empowering. It moves you from a passive state, where life happens to you, to an active state, where you are in control of your destiny. You are taking a steady, clear-sighted, introspective look at your life, understanding your weaknesses, and confronting uncomfortable truths. This level of self-awareness is essential for your personal growth.

You are laying the foundation for strategic planning because once you acknowledge your Black Dots, you can start to develop strategies and tactics to address them. This acknowledgment serves as the foundation for planning and action. Without recognizing these challenges, it would be challenging to formulate an effective plan to overcome them.

You are experiencing a powerful motivation for Change. Defining your Black Dots is a powerful catalyst that motivates you to seek solutions, acquire new skills, or make necessary life changes. It sparks your journey of transformation.

Acknowledging the challenges you face is an emotional process. It involves accepting not just the existence of problems but also the feelings associated with them: frustration, fear, disappointment—these are negative emotions, which partly explains why up until this point you might have been pushing the problems away and not dealing with them. That suppression can lead to stress, anxiety, and dissatisfaction.

Acknowledging a Black Dot is the first step to addressing underlying issues. Once you accept the feelings linked to the problems, your emotional acceptance becomes the key to developing resilience and a positive mindset to deal with the problems.

Recognizing your Black Dots brings clarity to what specific areas of your life need attention. It helps you to prioritize issues based on their impact and how urgent they are. In turn, this allows for a more focused approach to solving the problems you face.

You are increasing your skills in solving problems. When you acknowledge your Black Dots, you can begin to analyze and understand them. In turn, that means you are defining problems and challenges that, until now, were not totally obvious. This new understanding is key to developing effective strategies to overcome the challenges.

And then, each time you acknowledge and tackle a Black Dot, you build your resilience. Acknowledgment begins to strengthen your ability to handle future challenges.

Acknowledging your Black Dots is empowering. It signifies taking control of your life rather than being passive or reactive to circumstances. It's a proactive step towards self-improvement and empowerment. It sets the foundation for your personal and professional growth because you are making a commitment to bettering yourself and your circumstances.

And because you are acknowledging the Black Dots in both your professional and your personal life, you are now starting a journey of holistic life improvement which should lead to a more balanced, fulfilled, and purposeful life.

And don't forget, your progress has an impact on other people: Your acknowledgment and handling of your Black Dots will serve as inspiration for others. It shows them that challenges can be faced and overcome.

Acknowledging the existence of black dots is about facing reality, understanding your current situation, and preparing yourself for the journey of overcoming these challenges. It's a critical step in transitioning from a passive state to an active and engaged approach in your personal development.

In summary, acknowledging the existence of Black Dots is essential. It's the first, and perhaps most important, step in transforming challenges into opportunities for growth and success. It's a declaration that you are ready to face and conquer the obstacles in your path.

Self-awareness is key to identifying your Black Dots

Self-awareness is a critical component of the Black Dot Philosophy. It plays a vital role in identifying and overcoming challenges (Black Dots) in one's life. It is a key factor in identifying black dots.

Self-awareness is something to be nurtured and practiced. Self-aware individuals often engage in regular reflection and introspection. This practice enables you to examine your life experiences and identify patterns or recurring issues that might represent black dots. Regularly assessing your overall life satisfaction is a part of being self-aware. Persistent dissatisfaction in certain life areas might signal the presence of black dots.

Self-aware people are open to feedback from others. Sometimes, insights from friends, family, or colleagues can help you recognize black dots that you might not have seen.

A self-aware person tends to be conscious of their physical and mental health. Persistent issues in these areas can be indicative of black dots in your life.

These features of self-awareness will help you to identify your Black Dots:

1. Being emotionally aware
2. Reflecting and engaging in regular introspection
3. Understanding your triggers
4. Knowing your values and priorities
5. Being open to feedback
6. Knowing your own goals
7. Being conscious of your physical and mental health
8. Assessing your satisfaction with your life overall.

Once you have used self-awareness to identify your Black Dots, the following benefits flow:

Understanding of emotional triggers
● Being self-aware means you can identify what triggers negative emotions or stress, which are often signs of underlying Black Dots. Understanding these triggers is crucial for addressing the root causes of your challenges.

Alignment of actions with values
● Self-awareness allows you to align your actions and decisions with your core values. This alignment is essential for tackling Black Dots that conflict with your values and goals.

Enhancement of decision-making
● With self-awareness, you can make more informed decisions that reflect your true desires and aspirations. This clarity is crucial when navigating the complexities of Black Dots.

THE BLACK DOT PHILOSOPHY

Personal growth and development

● Self-awareness is the foundation of personal growth. By understanding yourself better, you can develop strategies that play to your strengths and address your weaknesses.

Improvement of relationships

● Self-awareness also improves your relationships. Understanding your own emotions helps you empathize with others, making it easier to navigate interpersonal Black Dots.

Creation of effective coping strategies

● Being self-aware enables you to develop coping strategies that are effective for your unique personality and situation. This is essential for overcoming challenges in a healthy and productive way.

Building resilience

● Self-awareness builds resilience by helping you understand how you react to adversity. Recognizing your patterns of behavior in challenging times is key to developing resilience.

Goal-setting and achievement

● Self-aware individuals are better equipped to set and achieve goals. Being aware of your personal goals and aspirations helps you identify when certain challenges or obstacles are hindering your progress towards these aims. These hindrances are your black dots. Understanding your Black Dots, your strengths, and your limitations helps in creating realistic and achievable goals.

Mindfulness and presence

● Self-awareness is closely linked to mindfulness. Being mindful and present in the moment can help you navigate Black Dots more effectively, as you're better attuned to the nuances of each challenge.

SUMMARY

Self-awareness is the starting point for effectively managing and overcoming the Black Dots in your life. It empowers you to take control of your journey, understand your challenges deeply, and navigate them with clarity and purpose. By cultivating self-awareness, you gain a clearer understanding of the challenges and obstacles in your life, allowing you to tackle them proactively. This process is fundamental in the Black Dot Philosophy, as it sets the stage for personal growth and overcoming life's hurdles.

We can change how we think about problems

The mindset shift required for embarking on the Black Dot journey is a fundamental change in how one perceives and approaches challenges. It's about transforming your outlook to see obstacles not as insurmountable problems but as opportunities for growth and development.

Let me elaborate on the key aspects of this mindset shift:

From Victim to Victor mentality

Instead of seeing oneself as a victim of circumstances, this shift involves adopting a winner's perspective. It means recognizing that you have the power and agency to confront and overcome your challenges.

From Fear to Courage

Many people are held back by fear, especially when facing their black dots. The mindset shift involves replacing fear with courage. It means acknowledging your fears but not letting them dictate your actions. Instead, you face your fears head-on.

From Fixed to Growth mindset

In a fixed mindset, people believe that their abilities and qualities are static and cannot be changed. The Black Dot Philosophy encourages a shift to a growth mindset, where you believe in your capacity to learn, adapt, and grow. Challenges are seen as opportunities for growth rather than as limitations.

From Doubt to Belief

Doubt and self-limiting beliefs can hinder progress. The mindset shift involves replacing doubt with belief in yourself and your potential. It means cultivating self-confidence and self-assurance.

From Short-term to Long-term thinking

Sometimes, we focus on short-term gains at the expense of long-term success. The mindset shift encourages thinking beyond immediate gratification and prioritizing long-term goals and sustainability.

From Blame to Responsibility

Instead of blaming external factors or others for your challenges, this shift involves taking responsibility for your life and your choices. It's about recognizing that you have control over your decisions and actions.

From Negative to Positive outlook

Shifting from a negative outlook to a positive one can have a profound impact. It means reframing challenges as opportunities, maintaining a hopeful attitude, and focusing on solutions rather than problems.

From Comfort zone to Growth zone

Many people stay in their comfort zones, avoiding discomfort and challenges. The mindset shift requires stepping out of this comfort zone and embracing discomfort as a catalyst for growth.

SUMMARY

The mindset shift required by the Black Dot Philosophy is about adopting a proactive, empowered, and growth-oriented perspective. It's about taking ownership of your life, believing in your potential, and approaching challenges with courage and resilience. This shift lays the foundation for turning challenges into triumphs and navigating life's journey more effectively.

How Black Dots transformed other peoples' lives

Let me share with you some real-life stories that highlight the transformative power of the Black Dot Philosophy. Each person faced different challenges and problems, but they found a way to confront and overcome their Black Dots and, in the process, showed their resilience and determination.

Sarah's health challenges

Sarah was a young professional who struggled with a chronic health condition that significantly affected her daily life and work. Her Black Dot was her health issue, which often left her feeling powerless and frustrated. By acknowledging this challenge, Sarah sought professional medical help, adjusted her lifestyle, and started a support group for others with similar conditions.

Through her journey, she not only improved her health but also found a new purpose in helping others, turning her challenge into a triumph.

Michael's career transition

Michael was in a high-paying job that he found unfulfilling. His Black Dot was his career dissatisfaction. He took the courageous step of leaving his secure job to pursue his passion for teaching. This required going back to school for a teaching degree and starting at a lower salary. However, his commitment to his true calling led him to a much more fulfilling career, showing how facing a black dot can lead to finding one's true purpose.

Linda's entrepreneurial leap

Linda had always dreamed of starting her own business but was held back by fear of failure. This fear was her Black Dot. After years in a stable but uninspiring corporate job, she finally decided to take the plunge. Despite initial setbacks, including financial challenges and learning curves, her persistence paid off. Her small home-based business eventually turned into a successful enterprise.

Linda's story exemplifies how confronting the fear that manifests as a black dot can lead to realizing one's entrepreneurial dreams.

John's battle with addiction

John's Black Dot was his struggle with alcohol addiction which was damaging his relationships and career. Recognizing this, he sought help through rehabilitation and therapy. It was a challenging journey filled with ups and downs but, through resilience and support, he overcame his addiction.

John's triumph over his Black Dot significantly improved his quality of life and relationships.

Emma's academic aspirations

Emma faced significant financial and societal challenges that made her academic aspirations seem unattainable: her Black Dot. However, through hard work, scholarships, and part-time jobs, she managed to enroll in university. Her journey was tough, balancing work and studies, but her determination and commitment to her goals paid off when she graduated with honors.

Each of these people could only start to transform their challenges into opportunities for growth and success once they identified and acknowledged their Black Dots. It was their resilience, determination, and strategic action that enabled them to overcome their individual adversity and achieve remarkable triumphs. Their examples are a testament to the human spirit's capacity to transform and I offer them as proof that whatever faces you, you can tackle your own Black Dots too.

Use this guide to identify your Black Dots

Identifying your Black Dots is your first step in applying the Black Dot Philosophy to your own life. First, I will give you ten principles that will help you to find your Black Dots, and then I will show you how to map them out, so that you have a visual reference to work with. Let me guide you through the process.

These are the ten principles to help you identify your Black Dots:

1. **Self-reflection and awareness**
   Begin with introspection. Reflect on your current state. What is troubling you right now? Now think about the different areas of your life—personal, professional, health, relationships, and so on. Ask yourself where you feel unfulfilled, stressed, or face recurring problems. These areas are likely where your Black Dots exist.

2. **Identify patterns**
   Look for patterns in your challenges. Do certain types of situations or behaviors consistently lead to problems or

dissatisfaction? Recognizing these patterns can help you pinpoint specific Black Dots.

3. **Listen to feedback**

   Sometimes, it's hard to see our own Black Dots. Listen to feedback from friends, family, and colleagues. They can provide insights into challenges you may not have recognized.

4. **Journaling**

   Keep a journal to track your daily experiences, thoughts, and feelings. This can be a powerful tool to identify recurring issues that might be your Black Dots.

5. **Assess life satisfaction**

   Periodically assess your satisfaction in various aspects of your life. Dissatisfaction can be a clear indicator of a Black Dot.

6. **Physical and emotional signals**

   Pay attention to physical and emotional signals. Stress, anxiety, or physical discomfort can be signs of unresolved Black Dots.

7. **Prior experiences**

   Reflect on past experiences and how they have shaped your current situation. Often, our present challenges are rooted in past experiences.

8. **Seek professional insight**

   Sometimes, it might be helpful to seek insight from a coach, therapist, or mentor. They can provide objective perspectives and help you uncover hidden Black Dots.

9. **Use visualization techniques**

   Visualize different aspects of your life and notice where you feel tension or unease. Visualization can help bring subconscious challenges to the surface.

10. Set aside assumptions

Be open to discovering Black Dots in unexpected areas of your life. Sometimes, we overlook challenges because we assume they are "normal" or "unavoidable."

Once you've identified your Black Dots, you can begin to address them systematically. We will look at this in more detail in the next section: *Mapping your Black Dots.*

Remember, the goal is not just to solve problems but to transform these challenges into opportunities for growth and success. Identifying your Black Dots is a step towards empowering yourself to live a more fulfilled life.

....

Map your Black Dots

Now that you have thought about the challenges you face, your "Black Dots," and started to identify them, you should map them out. Mapping your Black Dots helps you systematically to identify them in tangible form.

It's a practical approach where you lay out these challenges in a structured format, making them easier to analyze. When you use a physical board or a digital tool to map out each challenge as a black dot, the visual presentation shows you all the obstacles you face and provides a clear overview of what needs to be addressed.

As you work on this, you will categorize each Black Dot based on its nature and impact. Categories might be personal, professional, health-related, financial, or emotional challenges. Maybe you can think of others. By categorizing, you can see patterns and how different challenges may be interconnected.

Once the Black Dots are mapped and categorized, your next step is to prioritize them. This means assessing which challenges are the most critical to address first, based on factors like urgency, impact on your life, and your ability to influence them.

With a clear view of your challenges, you can then start to strategize how to tackle each one. This might involve setting specific goals, identifying resources needed, and planning actionable steps.

Your map is not static; it's a dynamic tool. As you start to work on your Black Dots, you update the map to reflect your progress, changes, or new challenges that arise. This ongoing process helps keep you focused and motivated.

The map also serves as a reflective tool that allows you to look back and see how far you've come in addressing your challenges. Use it as a source of motivation and a reminder of your resilience and ability to overcome obstacles.

Over time, your Black Dot map becomes a valuable resource for understanding how you deal with challenges. It will guide you when you need to tackle future obstacles, and it will help you do it more effectively.

When you map your Black Dots, you are empowering yourself to take control of your challenges. You will understand them more deeply and approach them with a structured and strategic mindset. It's about transforming the abstract concept of the challenges facing you into something concrete and manageable.

This is how to map your Black Dots

Creating a visual representation of your Black Dots is a powerful exercise that can help you connect your challenges to your life's purpose. You will need one sheet of paper to make a list, and another, larger sheet of paper, or a whiteboard, or a digital tool, to draw your map.

Here's a step-by-step guide to help you through this process.

1. **Identify Your Black Dots**

   Begin by listing your current challenges or obstacles on the smaller sheet of paper. These can be related to various aspects of your life, such as career, relationships, health, personal growth, or finances. Write them down as succinctly as possible.

2. **Create a Visual Map**

   Turn to the large sheet of paper, or the whiteboard, or the digital tool, to create your map. Represent each challenge as a black dot and place them on the map. This is a good moment to think about the nature of each Black Dot and what impact it is having on you. Categorize each Black Dot, using symbols, or colors, or sizes to indicate the nature or severity of each challenge.

3. **Define Your Life's Purpose**

   In a blank space on your map, write down a statement, or a few words that encapsulate your life's purpose. This could be something like "Empowering others through education" or "Living a life of creativity and innovation." Your purpose should reflect your core values and what you find most meaningful. (If you are finding it difficult to define your purpose, take a look at the section in this book called *Understand your Purpose*.)

4. **Draw Connections**

   Now, draw lines or arrows connecting each Black Dot to your purpose statement. As you do this, reflect on how each challenge relates to your purpose. Ask yourself, "How does overcoming this challenge align with, or contribute to, my life's purpose?"

5. **Prioritize and Strategize**

   Look at the connections you've made and prioritize your black dots based on how significantly they impact your purpose. For the more critical challenges, start brainstorming strategies and actions that can help you address them in a way that furthers your purpose. (We will take a long hard look at how to develop strategies that achieve your goals in a later section of this book).

6. **Reflect on Interconnectedness**
   Take a step back and observe the interconnectedness of your challenges and purpose. Notice if addressing one challenge could positively impact another or bring you closer to your purpose.

7. **Update, Reflect, and Adjust**
   Your map is a living document. Set yourself reminders to reflect regularly on it because, as you progress and overcome challenges, or as your understanding of your purpose evolves, you will want to update your map. You may discover new challenges. You might redefine your life's purpose. Keeping your map front of mind will help you stay aligned with your purpose and adapt to new challenges.

By visually mapping out your black dots in relation to your life's purpose, you can gain a clearer understanding of how your challenges shape your journey. This exercise not only helps in strategizing how to tackle each obstacle but also ensures that your actions are aligned with your deeper life goals. It's a powerful way to maintain focus and motivation and ensures that every step you take is purpose-driven.

Exercises to help identify your Black Dots

Self-awareness is the starting point for effectively managing and overcoming the Black Dots in your life. Here are a variety of ways to enhance self-awareness and facilitate the identification of personal challenges and goals.

Journaling

Regularly write in a journal, reflecting on your daily experiences, thoughts, and feelings. This practice can reveal patterns in your behavior and emotions, helping you identify your black dots.

Mindfulness Meditation

Practice mindfulness meditation to stay present and aware of your thoughts and emotions. This can help you gain insight into your subconscious mind and understand your internal challenges.

Ask Self-Reflective Questions

Ask yourself introspective questions such as, "What are my core values?", "What gives me a sense of fulfillment?", or "What are my fears, and how do they impact my choices?" Answering these can lead to revelations about your Black Dots. (Later in this book, you will find a long list of questions that help to promote self-discovery.)

Strengths and Weaknesses Assessment

Identify your strengths and weaknesses, perhaps by using self-assessment tools, or seeking feedback from others. This understanding helps in recognizing areas where you excel and where you face challenges.

Visualization Exercises

Engage in guided visualization to picture your ideal future or to confront your challenges. Visualize overcoming your Black Dots and achieving your goals.

Emotional Tracking

Keep a log of your emotions and what triggers them throughout the day. This can help you identify patterns and potential black dots related to your emotional responses.

Life Wheel Exercise

Draw a life wheel, dividing it into sections representing different life areas such as, your career, relationships, health, and so on. Rate your satisfaction in each area to identify where your Black Dots may lie.

Values Clarification

List your core values and reflect on how well your current life aligns with these values. Misalignments can point to significant black dots.

Goal-setting

Set specific, measurable, achievable, relevant, and time-bound (SMART) goals. Regularly review and adjust these goals to ensure they align with your evolving understanding of your black dots.

Mindfulness and Presence

Self-awareness is closely linked to mindfulness. When you are present in the moment, you are able to appreciate the nuances of each of your challenges and that helps you to navigate your Black Dots more effectively.

Seek Feedback

Ask for honest feedback from friends, family, or colleagues about your strengths and areas for improvement. This external perspective can help you uncover black dots you might not be aware of.

Past Life Events Analysis

Reflect on significant past events and the lessons you have learned from them. When you understand how these events shaped you, you can highlight areas for future growth.

Create Bucket Lists

Compile a list of experiences or achievements you aspire to. This can shed light on your deepest desires and potential black dots that might be holding you back.

Personality Assessments

Consider taking personality tests like the Myers-Briggs Type Indicator or the Big Five Personality Traits to gain deeper insights into your personality and potential black dots.

Gratitude Practice

Regularly practice gratitude, focusing on the positive aspects of your life. This can shift your perspective and help identify areas of dissatisfaction.

Limiting Belief Identification

Recognize and challenge any limiting beliefs you hold about yourself. These beliefs can be significant black dots, blocking your path to growth and fulfillment.

SUMMARY

These exercises to increase your self-awareness are most effective when done regularly and with honest introspection. As they guide you through the process of self-discovery, they will help you to identify and confront the black dots in your life. With practice, you can take control of your journey and understand your challenges deeply so that you navigate them with clarity and purpose.

No Black Dot is the same size as another

In the Black Dot Philosophy, the concept of Black Dots as challenges to overcome and goals to achieve is central. You won't have just one

Black Dot; you will identify multiple Black Dots in the near future of your life.

Let's look at your Black Dot map. The dots should vary in size and significance because each one represents part of a diverse range of obstacles and aspirations that you face today.

Take a closer look at how big you have made each of those dots. Remember, a Black Dot is a metaphor for the magnitude of a challenge or goal. Adjust yours so that they vary in size in relation to each other and in relation to how much energy, how long and what you need to deal with it.

Size

The size of a Black Dot indicates the amount of effort, time, and resources that might be needed to address it. So, for important life challenges, such as career transitions, health issues, relationship issues, or major life decisions, you'll draw a larger dot. Use smaller dots to symbolize everyday hurdles or minor goals, like improving a skill or resolving a routine conflict.

Significance

The significance of a black dot can vary depending on its impact on an individual's life and their personal or professional growth. Some dots might have profound long-term implications that deeply affect your life trajectory, while others might influence more immediate or short-term aspects.

Personal context

The size of a Black Dot does not only relate to the objective magnitude of the challenge, where, for example, a diagnosis of serious illness is objectively a bigger issue than an ongoing power struggle between two junior members of your team. You will also want to judge its relative significance to your own life and your personal or professional growth.

So, if we were to look at two different managers of a team where that power struggle between junior members is going on, the manager who suffers severe emotional stress might represent the issue by a larger Black Dot than the manager who is less personally impacted by the struggle. Thus, a challenge that appears as a large dot for one individual might be a small dot for another, depending on their unique circumstances, skills, and resources.

Dynamic Nature
Black dots are not static: They can change in size and significance over time. As individuals grow, learn, and adapt, what once seemed like a large and daunting dot can shrink in size. Conversely, problems can increase in significance due to circumstances outside our control.

Multiplicity of Dots
It's common to have multiple black dots present at any given time and each one represents different challenges or goals. The thing you are going to have to do is to manage these simultaneously and that requires both prioritization and a great strategy. I'm going to show you how to do that, later in the book.

Visual Representation
As you read this, you are probably beginning to see that visualizing challenges and goals as black dots provides a clear and tangible way to acknowledge and address them. It's going to help you map out a plan of action and track progress as dots are reduced in size or wiped out.

Not all Black Dots are challenges
Some Black Dots represent goals or aspirations. When you clear them off your plan of action, you are signifying your achievement and success, and that contributes to a sense of accomplishment and personal growth.

The concept of Black Dots in the Black Dot Philosophy is a versatile and effective tool for representing and managing life's varied challenges and goals. When you use Black Dots as a metaphor, you are emphasizing the importance of awareness, prioritization, and proactive engagement in your own personal development and problem-solving.

Prioritize your Black Dots

Prioritizing black dots based on their significance is a crucial aspect of the Black Dot Philosophy. It's about recognizing that not all challenges have the same impact on your life or align equally with your goals.

We will look harder at how you should prioritize action to deal with your Black Dots in the next section of this book, when you will look harder at how your Black Dots align with your purpose in life. But here, I want to explain why it is essential to prioritize.

Doing so, allows you to allocate your resources effectively. We all have limited time, energy, and resources. By prioritizing your Black Dots, you can focus your efforts on the challenges that will have the most significant impact. This ensures that you're not expending valuable resources on less critical issues.

Prioritization helps to clear the clutter. When you identify which black dots are most significant, you gain clarity on what requires your immediate attention. Clarity allows you to focus on dealing with that particular black dot; that focused attention is vital for developing targeted strategies and avoiding feeling overwhelmed.

Not all black dots require the same approach. Prioritizing allows you to tailor your problem-solving methods appropriately. More significant black dots might need a more comprehensive, long-term strategy, while smaller ones might be resolved with quicker, simpler solutions.

Tackling the most significant black dots can lead to noticeable improvements in your life, which boosts motivation. Each time you overcome a major challenge, it builds momentum, encouraging you to address the next one.

Prioritizing black dots ensures that your actions are aligned with your long-term goals and values. By focusing on what matters most, you are more likely to find success and fulfillment in your endeavors.

In essence, the process of prioritizing black dots is about making strategic choices. It involves assessing the impact, urgency, and alignment of each challenge with your overall goals. By doing so, you can navigate your life more effectively, ensuring that your efforts are concentrated where they will yield the greatest benefits.

Prioritization is not just about managing challenges; it's about steering your life in the direction that aligns with your vision and purpose.

Know your Black Dots to enhance your goal-setting

When you identify a black dot, you have taken the first step towards thinking about how overcome a challenge. Once you have clearly identified it, you can start to set goals that are not just wishful thinking but are rooted in real, tangible issues or aspirations. When you know exactly what your Black Dots are, you can set goals that directly address them.

We will look at the art of goal-setting in more detail later in the book, but let's take a moment to think about half-a-dozen ways in which being clear about your Black Dots will help you to set achievable goals.

Aligning Goals with Personal Values and Purpose

By gaining clarity on your black dots, you can align your goals with your personal values and overall life purpose. This alignment ensures that your goals are meaningful and resonate deeply with you which is crucial for long-term commitment and motivation.

Prioritization of Goals

Understanding your black dots helps you to prioritize which challenges to tackle first. This prioritization is essential for effective goal-setting as it helps you focus on the most critical issues first, ensuring efficient use of your time and resources.

Setting Realistic and Achievable Goals

Clarity about the nature and extent of your black dots enables you to set realistic and achievable goals. When you have a thorough understanding of the challenges you face, you can set goals that are challenging yet within reach, increasing the likelihood of success.

Creating a Focused Plan of Action

With clear black dots, you can develop a more focused and structured plan of action. This plan can include specific strategies and tactics to address each Black Dot, making your goal-setting process more strategic and results-oriented.

Measuring Progress and Success

Clarity about your black dots provides a clear benchmark against which to measure progress. You can set specific milestones and indicators of success related to each Black Dot, allowing you to track your progress effectively and make adjustments as needed.

Building Confidence and Motivation

Achieving clarity on your black dots and setting focused goals can build confidence. As you start to tackle each Black Dot effectively, your belief in your ability to overcome challenges and achieve your goals strengthens, further fueling your motivation.

SUMMARY

Clarity about one's Black Dots leads to more focused and effective goal-setting by enabling specific, aligned, prioritized, realistic, and structured goals. This clarity is a powerful tool in the Black Dot Philosophy, helping you to not only set but also achieve meaningful and impactful goals in your life.

Turning your Black Dots into actionable goals

As I said before, we will take the time to look hard at Goal-Setting later in the book. Now, I'd like to give you a preview of the power that lies in this work to address your Black Dots: the challenges, or obstacles, in your personal and professional life.

Turning black dots into actionable goals is a transformative process in the Black Dot Philosophy. Once you have identified your Black Dots and analyzed each one to understand its nature and impact (an understanding that is critical in transforming these challenges into goals) and prioritized them based on their significance in your life, then you will want to develop actionable goals so that you can work towards addressing each Black Dot.

For each Black Dot, create specific, measurable, achievable, relevant, and time-bound (SMART) goals. For instance, if a black dot is related to fitness, an actionable goal could be, "I will exercise for 30 minutes, five days a week, for the next three months to improve my cardiovascular health."

For each goal, develop strategies (the overarching plan) and tactics (specific actions). Using the fitness goal as an example, a strategy could be adopting a holistic approach to health, while tactics might include scheduling workouts, planning nutritious meals, and tracking progress. We will look at strategies and tactics in a lot more detail later in the book.

Put your strategies and tactics into action so that you move towards each goal. Regular review and adjustment may be necessary based on your progress and any new insights that emerge.

Regularly assess how well you're meeting your goals. Are your strategies and tactics effective? Be prepared to adjust your plans as needed.

Recognize and celebrate your progress. Each step forward, no matter how small, is a triumph in converting a black dot into a successful outcome.

Reflect on the journey of transforming each Black Dot into a goal. What did you learn? How have you grown?

Repeat the process. The Black Dot Philosophy is an ongoing journey. As you overcome one set of black dots, new ones are likely to emerge. Repeat the process with these new challenges, continually growing and evolving.

SUMMARY

By transforming black dots into actionable goals, you're not just overcoming challenges; you're actively shaping your life's trajectory. This process empowers you to turn obstacles into opportunities for growth and fulfillment.

People who have made this work for them

Let's look at a few examples of individuals who faced significant black dots and turned them into remarkable triumphs:

Maria's Career Shift

Maria was a successful lawyer but felt unfulfilled in her corporate job. Her Black Dot was her dissatisfaction with her career. She took the bold step of leaving her job to pursue her passion for environmental activism. It was a risky move, but she used strategic planning, networking, and continuous learning to establish herself in the new field. Today, Maria runs a successful non-profit organization focused on environmental protection, feeling more fulfilled than ever.

Alex's Health Transformation

Alex faced a significant health challenge—morbid obesity. This Black Dot was affecting his physical health, self-esteem, and overall quality of life. He set a goal to exercise following a particular regimen. Despite setbacks and challenges, Alex stayed committed. Over two years, he lost more than 100 pounds and significantly improved his health. His journey inspired others in his community to prioritize their health.

Samantha's Educational Pursuit

Samantha grew up in a low-income neighborhood with limited educational opportunities. Her black dot was the lack of access to quality education. Determined to break the cycle, she worked multiple jobs to fund her education. With perseverance and hard work, she earned a scholarship to a prestigious university. Samantha's success story became a beacon of hope for many in her community.

Liam's Small Business Success

Liam's Black Dot was his struggling small business which was close to bankruptcy. He reassessed his business model, identified new market opportunities, and rebranded his offerings. Liam also embraced digital marketing to reach a broader audience. His efforts paid off, and his business not only survived but thrived, expanding into new markets.

Nina's Artistic Breakthrough

Nina, a talented artist, faced the Black Dot of not being recognized for her work. She took the initiative to create an online portfolio and actively networked in local art communities. Her persistence paid off when her art was featured in a major exhibition, leading to critical acclaim and commercial success.

Each of these individuals faced their Black Dots head-on. They used strategic thinking, demonstrated resilience and commitment, and ultimately achieved success and fulfillment. Their stories illustrate the essence of the Black Dot Philosophy. Like them, you will identify your challenges, set goals to deal with them, and methodically work towards your goals following a path to transformative outcomes.

Think about your own Black Dot journey

We have considered the importance of recognizing Black Dots in life, and you probably now have a good understanding of the subtlety of life's challenges. Black Dots are real, and they exist. This book is here to help you deal with them.

To help you embed the Philosophy into your own outlook, I suggest you do this:

- Write down your personal definition of the Black Dot Philosophy
- Reflect on the significance of challenges in your life
- Set an initial Black Dot goal for yourself.

Take a moment to think about how your life might change by embracing the Black Dot Philosophy, and then:

- List three challenges or obstacles you currently face
- Reflect on whether these challenges are Black Dots
- Consider how these Black Dots might be affecting your life
- Write down your thoughts on how identifying your Black Dots can lead to positive changes.

STEP
2

CHART YOUR COURSE

As mentioned earlier, I really struggled on and off in my first couple of years at New York Life. I was not only new to the company and its culture but also relatively new to the Bay Area and didn't know many people. Since recruiting was my number one job as a Partner, it was a real disadvantage.

Additionally, most advisors who transition into a leadership role are typically promoted after a few years of building their own book of business. It's a huge advantage to be able to tap into your book of business to find high-quality candidates, but once you start to build a team, your book of business could also generate sales for these new members of the team as once you become part of the leadership team you are no longer permitted to sell products for your own benefit. You had no choice but to give that business to deserving members of your team! Since I wasn't an advisor for the company and hired directly into management, at was at a huge disadvantage.

So I had to think outside the box as it related to sourcing names in order to find, interview, and hire quality candidates. I also needed to come up with some creative ideas to help generate sales for my new hires. Naturally, I used my newfound process and system, The Black Dot Philosophy, to meet and ultimately exceed all company expectations. But I wasn't looking to meet or exceed expectations—I was determined to be eligible for promotion by the end of my fourth year with the company. I needed to chart my own course using The Black Dot Philosophy. I needed to crush my competition within the company so I would be a natural choice to run my own agency.

Each year, there were only a handful of open offices due to death, disability, terminations, or retirements. The company had a promotability index they used to rank eligible managers, and if you weren't ranked at the very top of the eligibility list, it was highly unlikely you were going to be asked to manage one of the 100+ offices they had throughout the country.

I will give you an example of how I used the Black Dot Philosophy to get promoted without any real contacts or a clientele to Managing Partner by my fourth year with the company.

Recruiting and retaining high-quality candidates to sell the company's products and services was the key to getting promoted. If I hired high-quality people who were dialed into their communities and they produced at a high level with my help, I could build a "team" of successful advisors fairly quickly. One of the most important factors is the total production your team produced in the 12-month period prior to the promotability index being published.

So the largest Black Dot for me at that time was getting promoted to Managing Partner. Quite frankly, it was all I thought about, and I was determined!

I want to also share with you that I had an even bigger "Black Dot" challenge and goal that I was also very determined to achieve.

That big, hairy, audacious Black Dot goal was to earn $1,000,000 or more by the time I turned 50. I had just turned 35 when I started with the company, so the goal was to earn $1,000,000 or more by 2008!

I'll get to that later in the book, but for now, I will share some of my Black Dot game plan to get promoted to Managing Partner. This gives you some perspective as to how The Black Dot Philosophy started to evolve shortly after I decided to develop it into a process-driven tool for both professional and personal challenges and goals. Here is a snapshot of what it looked like:

- The Black Dot (goal): Get promoted to Managing Partner no later than my 4th year with the company.
- Strategy #1: Hire 8-10 quality candidates as early in the year as possible to get the most production possible from my current class.
- Tactics:
  1. Focus on experienced advisors who already have experience and a book of business.
  2. Request lunch meetings with our successful and experienced advisors with large books of business for referrals.
  3. Recruit to management opportunity. Utilize the company's fast-track management program to hire future management candidates.
  4. Meet with Athletic Directors at local colleges and universities to get names of star athletes who recently graduated and did not turn professional. Collegiate Athletes were and still are great candidates for careers in the Financial Services Industry.
  5. Implement a targeted direct mail campaign to professionals earning between $50,000 - $100,000 who have hit the glass ceiling in their current career.

I not only met my recruiting objective, but I also hired the majority of candidates early in the year, which means that class was very productive. So in combination with the advisors I hired and retained from the Recruiting Classes of the three previous years, the team's production and other components used to calculate the promotability index were enough to put me at the top of the index. In summer of the following year, I got the call to manage the Central Coast General Office. I was now responsible for growth in the coastal communities of Ventura, Santa Barbara, and San Luis Obispo counties in Southern and Central California. That said, it was also one of the worst offices for a variety of reasons in the entire country. It was like walking into a firestorm. I would have my work cut out for me. Be careful what you wish for; you just might get it!

Purpose, Discipline, and Goals

In the Black Dot Philosophy, your purpose, your discipline, and your goals are interlinked and are essential components of personal growth and success.

Purpose provides motivation and direction, *Discipline* ensures consistent action and accountability, and *Goals* offer a clear path to achievement and measurable outcomes. Together, they form a powerful framework for navigating life's challenges. They can transform them into opportunities, enabling you to achieve both personal and professional success.

In this section, we are going to look hard at each of these three elements, and then we are going to see how you can make Purpose, Discipline, and Goals work together to facilitate your personal and professional growth.

Align your actions with your Purpose

As we dig deeper into understanding the Power of Purpose, you will learn about the importance of identifying your core motivations and how these underpin your actions and decisions. I will help you explore how aligning your everyday actions with your purpose can lead to more meaningful and focused efforts. And I will give you insights into how a strong sense of purpose can bolster resilience, especially when facing significant challenges, your Black Dots.

Discipline will keep you going to the end

Discipline is the key to maintaining consistency in taking action to address your Black Dots. We will look at some strategies for building and maintaining discipline, crucial for long-term success. We will look at the importance of the role of habits and routines; I will show you why disciplined habits and routines are essential in systematically addressing Black Dots and achieving goals. We will also cover the importance of accountability in maintaining discipline, along with practical ways to implement it.

Transform abstract challenges into actionable goals

Then we will move onto setting, and achieving, goals. We will delve into effective goal-setting techniques, using SMART criteria for making goals Specific, Measurable, Achievable, Relevant, and Time-Bound. We will look at how to transform abstract challenges into clear, actionable goals and we will consider the importance of tracking your progress towards your goals and the importance of celebrating your achievements so that you maintain your motivation.

Synergy of Purpose, Discipline, and Goals

We are then going to look at how purpose, discipline, and goals work synergistically to facilitate personal and professional growth.

SUMMARY

Through case studies and real-life examples, you will see how individuals have successfully applied these principles in overcoming their Black Dots, and you will find some exercises and reflection prompts to help you apply these concepts to your own life.

....

The Power of Purpose

Let's take a moment to review why having a clear sense of purpose matters. People with a strong sense of purpose tend to be more motivated, resilient, and fulfilled. A clear sense of purpose can have a profound impact on an individual's overall well-being and approach to life.

Knowing your purpose affords you:

- Direction and Motivation
- Resilience Through Challenges
- Fulfillment and Satisfaction

By way of example, my purpose in writing this part of this book is to help you explore and articulate your own purpose, so providing you with a framework for living a more focused, fulfilling, and impactful life.

Direction and Motivation

When you have a clear sense of your own Purpose, it gives you a sense of direction. It serves as a powerful, and intrinsic motivator. In the Black Dot Philosophy, understanding your *why*, the reason behind your actions, is crucial. When you can articulate your purpose in life, it naturally fuels your drive to pursue your goals and you can align your actions with your deeper values and motivations.

Resilience Through Challenges

When facing your Black Dots, knowing your purpose helps you to maintain resilience. People with a clear purpose are more likely to put in sustained effort towards their objectives. They are more likely to view difficulties as opportunities for growth and learning, which aids in quicker recovery from setbacks.

Even when the task is challenging, and obstacles seem insurmountable, a strong sense of purpose gives you a reason to persist and equips you to better handle adversity. When faced with setbacks or challenges, your purpose serves as an anchor, helping you to stay grounded and maintain perspective.

Fulfillment and Satisfaction

Pursuing goals that are aligned with one's purpose leads to greater fulfillment. It's not just about achieving objectives but about realizing a part of your identity and life mission.

While external achievements can bring temporary satisfaction, an inner sense of purpose offers deeper, more enduring fulfillment. It's not just about what you achieve, but how these achievements align with your inner values and beliefs. In turn, having a purpose provides a sense of meaning to one's life. This sense of meaning contributes significantly to your overall life satisfaction and well-being.

So, the concept of *purpose* is a fundamental guiding force in our lives. Purpose can be understood as the underlying *why* behind our actions and decisions—it's the driving force that gives direction and meaning to our existence.

In essence, a strong sense of purpose acts as a powerful driving force that imbues individuals with motivation, resilience, and a deep sense of fulfillment. It's not just a guiding principle for significant life decisions; it permeates all aspects of living, influencing daily actions, behaviors, and attitudes. This comprehensive impact of purpose is what makes it an essential element of a contented, motivated, and resilient life.

Let's take a closer look at this.

Purpose as the driving force

Purpose is often an intrinsic motivator that stems from our core values, beliefs, and passions. It's what inspires and compels us to act, even in the absence of external rewards.

Unlike temporary pleasures or external achievements, purpose offers a deeper sense of fulfillment. It's about being aligned with what we feel is our calling or mission in life.

Purpose in long-term decision-making

When we have a clear sense of purpose, our decisions tend to be more aligned with our long-term goals and values. This clarity helps in making choices that are consistent with our true selves.

Purpose influences our daily actions and habits

On a practical level, a strong sense of purpose influences our daily actions and habits. It shapes how we spend our time each day and the habits we cultivate. These daily decisions tend to be more aligned with long-term goals and personal values.

Purpose helps us prioritize

It helps in determining what is truly important to do in our life, and what is deserving of our time and resources.

Purpose gives us resilience

A strong sense of purpose can help us to overcome challenges and is a source of resilience in difficult times. When faced with obstacles or setbacks, a clear purpose can provide the strength and motivation to persevere.

Purpose enables us to maintain a long-term perspective, even when faced with immediate challenges. It allows us to see beyond the current situation and stay focused on our overarching goals.

Purpose aids our personal growth

Discovering one's purpose involves a journey of self-discovery. It requires introspection and a deep understanding of one's passions, talents, and values.

Purpose is not static; it can evolve and change as we grow and gain new experiences. This evolution is a natural part of personal growth and development.

The impact of a sense of purpose

Purpose extends beyond personal achievements to include making a positive impact on others and contributing to something larger than oneself.

Living a purpose-driven life can also be about the legacy we want to leave and the impact we want to have on the world.

Purpose helps us find our true goals

Purpose helps us to align our goals with our deeper motivations. Goals that are rooted in our purpose are more likely to be fulfilling and motivating. People with a clear purpose experience a higher quality of life. Their actions and choices are coherent with their overarching life goals, leading to a more harmonious and fulfilling existence.

SUMMARY

Purpose is the foundational *why* behind our existence. It's what gives our lives direction and meaning, influences our decisions, enables us to overcome challenges, and drives our personal growth and impact on the world.

The Search for Purpose

You may be thinking, "It's all very well to talk about bringing clarity to my sense of purpose but how do I actually define my purpose?"

This section addresses the common struggles many people face in defining a clear and meaningful purpose. It highlights how this struggle can lead to feelings of aimlessness, dissatisfaction, and a sense of not fully engaging with one's potential. This is why it is so important to discover and embrace one's purpose in order to lead a fulfilling and contented life.

Let's begin by acknowledging the difficulties associated with defining, and not defining your sense of purpose.

The challenges in defining purpose

Complexity and Depth

Defining one's purpose can be challenging because it involves delving into deep, introspective questions about one's values, passions, and aspirations. Many people find it difficult to articulate these inner motivations and how they translate into a life purpose.

External Influences

Societal expectations, cultural norms, and external pressures can cloud your understanding of your true purpose. People often get swayed by what they believe they should be doing rather than what they genuinely want to do.

Feelings of Aimlessness

Lack of Direction

Without a clear sense of purpose, one can experience feelings of aimlessness. This manifests as a lack of direction or uncertainty about where to focus your efforts and energies.

Difficulty in decision-making

A well-defined purpose acts as a guide for making decisions. Without it, you may struggle to make choices that are aligned with your long-term goals or personal values. In turn, that may lead to indecision and confusion.

Dissatisfaction and discontent

Misalignment with inner values

When actions and life paths are not aligned with one's intrinsic values and interests, it can lead to feelings of dissatisfaction. People may feel like they are not living up to their potential or not leading a life that is truly meaningful to them.

Unfulfilled potential

The lack of a clear purpose can prevent you from fully realizing your potential. You might engage in activities that don't fully utilize your talents or passions, leading to a sense of unfulfillment.

The Quest for meaning

Inherent human desire

Humans have an inherent desire to seek meaning and purpose in their lives. This quest for meaning is a fundamental aspect of human psychology and well-being.

Existential questions

Part of the struggle in finding your sense of purpose involves grappling with existential questions about one's role and contribution to the world. Such questions are daunting and complex.

Impact on mental and emotional health

The uncertainty and dissatisfaction arising from not knowing one's purpose can impact mental and emotional health. It can lead to feelings of stagnation, depression, or anxiety.

Find your purpose through introspection and self-discovery

Finding one's purpose requires introspection and self-discovery. I'm referring to the deep, reflective process you must engage in to understand your true motivations, values, and passions.

Introspection

Introspection involves looking inward and reflecting on your own thoughts, feelings, and motivations. Ask yourself profound questions like, "What brings me joy?", "What am I passionate about?", and "What do I value most in life?"

Part of introspection is analyzing your past experiences to identify moments when you felt most fulfilled or engaged. This can provide clues about your intrinsic motivations and potential purpose.

Self-Discovery

Self-discovery is about uncovering your personal, core values and beliefs. It's a process of understanding what truly matters to you, ignoring external influences or societal expectations that can cloud your true desires.

It also involves recognizing your strengths and passions. Discovering what you are naturally good at and what excites you can be key indicators of your purpose.

The journey to finding one's purpose can force you to confront inner fears, doubts, and barriers. This emotional and mental journey is crucial in breaking free from limitations and realizing your true potential.

Introspection and self-discovery help in distinguishing between what you think you should do and what you genuinely want to do. Practical methods like journaling, meditation, and mindfulness practices can facilitate the finding of your true purpose. They provide the space and structure for reflective thinking.

It's an evolving process

Finding one's purpose is not a one-time event but an evolving process. As you grow and change, so, too, can your purpose. It requires continual self-reflection and adaptation.

In essence, the process of finding one's purpose through introspection and self-discovery is about delving into the depths of your inner self to uncover what truly drives and fulfills you. It's a deeply personal journey that involves understanding your unique attributes, experiences, values, and passions. It is fundamental to living a purpose-driven and meaningful life.

The Importance of Self-reflection

Self-reflection plays a pivotal role in this process because it allows you to gain self-awareness, giving you a deeper understanding of your inner dynamics—your thoughts, feelings, motivations, and desires. It helps in uncovering what truly matters to you, separate from external influences.

Through self-reflection, you can identify your core values. These are essential components of one's purpose. Understanding what you stand for and what you believe in is crucial in defining your purpose.

Reflecting on past experiences, especially moments of deep satisfaction and engagement, can reveal your true passions. These passions often point towards areas where your purpose may lie.

Self-reflection allows you to recognize your unique strengths and talents. Often, your purpose aligns with what you are naturally good at and what brings you joy.

Self-reflection helps in identifying and confronting personal barriers, fears, and limiting beliefs. Understanding these obstacles is essential in overcoming them and moving towards your purpose.

Engaging in self-reflection is a process of personal growth. It involves challenging yourself, questioning your current state, and striving for a deeper understanding of your life's direction.

Self-reflection aids in clarifying your life goals. It ensures that the goals you set are genuinely aligned with your purpose and not dictated by external expectations.

It helps in prioritizing life choices based on what is truly important and meaningful to you, which is critical for living a purpose-driven life.

Through self-reflection, individuals can make more informed and thoughtful decisions. It provides a clearer perspective. This is essential for decision-making that resonates with your purpose.

Self-reflection cultivates mindfulness and a sense of presence. Being aware and present can lead to a more profound understanding of your purpose in life.

In summary, self-reflection is a vital tool in the journey towards discovering your purpose. It involves delving into your inner self to understand your motivations, values, passions, and strengths. This process is fundamental to aligning your life with a purpose that truly resonates with your authentic self.

How to integrate these practices into self-discovery and purpose-finding

I can't emphasize enough the importance of dedicating time to self-reflection.

Here's more detail on how these practices can be integrated into your journey of self-discovery and purpose-finding:

Journal for self-reflection

Daily reflection

I've already suggested practices like journaling and meditation as effective methods to help define your purpose.

Keeping a daily journal allows you to develop the habit of reflecting on your experiences, thoughts, and feelings. This practice can provide insights into your inner world and help identify recurring themes or patterns.

Use prompts

Use specific prompts to guide your journaling. Examples are:

- "What brought me joy today?"
- "What challenges did I face and how did I respond?"

Express gratitude

Including aspects of gratitude in journaling can shift your focus to positive experiences and personal growth areas. Examples are:

- "I am grateful to know [name] because they show me that…"
- "I am so lucky to have [XYZ] because it enables me to…"
- "Today, I told [name] how much I appreciated them because…"

Review your actions against your goals

Use your journaling to reflect on your personal goals and aspirations. Ask yourself, "How do my current actions align with these objectives?"

Meditate for self-reflection

Mindfulness meditation
Introduce mindfulness meditation into your daily routine to enhance your self-awareness. This form of meditation involves focusing on the present moment and observing your thoughts and feelings without judgment.

Guided meditation sessions
For beginners, guided meditation sessions can be beneficial. These can be accessed through apps, online platforms, or in-person classes.

Reflection post-meditation
After meditation, spend a few minutes reflecting on any insights or clarity that may have emerged regarding your personal purpose or goals. Jot down anything that strikes you as true in your journal.

Integrate your self-reflection into daily life

Dedicate a time
Set aside a specific time each day for meditation, starting with a few minutes and gradually increasing the duration, so that you form a strong habit.

Integrate into your routine
You are more likely to remember to do it if you integrate self-reflection into your existing daily routines, such as during morning rituals, evening wind-downs, or in breaks in the day.

Take reflective walks
When you take regular walks alone, you have the perfect opportunity to ponder your personal goals, challenges, and feelings.

Set up a reflective space

Dedicated space
The environment around you is an important influence on your reflective practice. Create a dedicated space for journaling and meditation that is quiet, comfortable, and free from distractions.

Reflective atmosphere
Elements like soft lighting, comfortable seating, and calming music, or recordings of nature sounds can enhance the quality of your reflection.

Review regularly
Set up a diary reminder, weekly or monthly to suit your circumstances, and be sure to turn up for yourself to review your journal entries and meditation insights. This way, you can track your progress, identify patterns, and make any necessary adjustments in your personal goals.

To recap, practices like journaling and meditation are essential tools for self-reflection in the journey towards discovering your purpose. These practices not only foster a deeper understanding of oneself but also help in aligning your daily actions with long-term aspirations and goals. By dedicating time to, and creating space for, these reflective practices, you can significantly enhance your self-awareness and clarity regarding your life's purpose.

Questions to spark self-discovery

Here is a list of thought-provoking questions designed to help you explore and identify your passions, values, and interests.

Passion exploration
» What activities make me lose track of time?
» When have I felt most alive and engaged in what I was doing?

» What topics do I find myself continuously drawn to read or learn about?

Value clarification

» What values are most important to me in life?
» When have I felt most proud of myself, and why?
» What actions or behaviors in others do I most admire?

Interest and joy

» What did I love to do as a child, and why did I stop?
» What brings me pure joy or a sense of peace?
» If I had an entire day to myself, how would I choose to spend it?

Talents and strengths

» What do others often compliment me on or seek my advice for?
» What are my natural talents or skills that come easily to me?
» In which areas do I feel most confident about my abilities?

Life goals and aspirations

» If I could achieve anything in life, what would it be?
» What would I regret not doing, being, or achieving in my life?
» What legacy do I want to leave behind?

Overcoming challenges

» What major challenges have I overcome in my life, and what did I learn from them?
» In difficult times, what beliefs or values keep me going?
» How do I define success, and have my definitions changed over time?

Personal growth and learning

» What skills or knowledge do I wish to acquire or improve?
» What areas of my life do I feel need more growth or development?
» How do I see myself evolving in the next five years?

Reflecting on relationships

» Who are the people I most admire, and what qualities do they possess?
» What kind of relationships do I want to cultivate or nurture more?
» In my relationships, what roles do I play, and are they fulfilling?

Career and professional aspirations

» What aspects of my current job or career do I find most fulfilling?
» If I could choose any career, regardless of money or talent, what would it be?
» What professional achievements would make me feel successful?

Contributing to the world

» What issues or causes am I passionate about?
» How do I want to make a difference in the world or my community?
» What does "making an impact" mean to me?

These questions are designed to prompt introspection and self-analysis, guiding you towards a deeper understanding of your inner self, your motivations, and your life's direction. They are meant to be pondered over time, with the understanding that self-discovery is an ongoing, evolving process.

Purpose-driven individuals

These examples of individuals in real life who have been driven by their sense of purpose to make an impact may inspire you to find your own deep purpose.

Muhammad Yunus—Social entrepreneurship

Nobel Peace Prize laureate Muhammad Yunus is known for founding the Grameen Bank and pioneering the concepts of microcredit and microfinance.

Purpose

His purpose was to combat poverty and empower the poor through providing small loans to those unable to access traditional banking services.

Impact

Yunus' innovative approach to social entrepreneurship has transformed the lives of millions of people, particularly women, in Bangladesh and around the world.

Temple Grandin—Advocate for autism and animal welfare

Temple Grandin, diagnosed with autism as a child, became one of the most influential people in the field of animal welfare and autism advocacy.

Purpose

Her purpose stemmed from her unique perspective on both autism and animal behavior, leading her to advocate for better livestock handling methods and understanding of autism.

Impact

Grandin revolutionized animal welfare in the livestock industry and has been a powerful voice in increasing awareness and understanding of autism.

Wangari Maathai—Environmental and political activism

Wangari Maathai was the first African woman to receive the Nobel Peace Prize for her contribution to sustainable development, democracy, and peace.

Purpose

Her purpose was rooted in environmental conservation and women's rights, leading her to found the Green Belt Movement in Kenya.

Impact

Maathai's work in planting over 50 million trees and advocating for environmental conservation and women's rights had a profound impact in Kenya and globally.

Paul Farmer—Global Health and Social Justice

Dr. Paul Farmer was a physician and anthropologist known for his humanitarian work providing healthcare to impoverished people.

Purpose

His purpose was to improve healthcare for the world's poorest populations, believing that access to healthcare is a fundamental right.

Impact

Farmer co-founded Partners In Health, an international organization that has brought quality healthcare to some of the most remote parts of the world.

Malala Yousafzai—Advocate for girls' education

As a young girl in Pakistan, Malala Yousafzai defied the Taliban by advocating for girls' education, leading to an assassination attempt.

Purpose

Her purpose was to promote education for all girls worldwide.

Impact

Surviving the attack, Malala became a global symbol for peaceful protest and was the youngest-ever Nobel Prize laureate.

Each of these individuals demonstrates how a clear sense of purpose can drive extraordinary efforts and lead to significant change. Their lives and work illustrate the power of purpose in guiding actions and creating meaningful impact in the world.

Take Action: Write Your Purpose Statement

It's time to draw together what you have learned so far. This ten-step guide will help you to articulate and write down your core values, your passions, and the impact you wish to have on the world. Follow it, step-by-step. Maybe you'd like to use your journal to work in, so that you know where to find it when you come to review it, again and again.

Step One: Reflect and prepare

Before writing your purpose statement, spend some time in reflection. Revisit the questions in the *Questions to Spark Self-Discovery* section and jot down your thoughts.

Step Two: Identify your core values

Make a list of your core values. These are the principles that are most important to you and guide your behavior. Choose the top three to five values that resonate deeply with you.

Step Three: Recognize your passions

Reflect on the activities, topics, or causes that you are deeply passionate about. Consider when you feel most alive and fulfilled. What are you doing during these times?

Step Four: Write down your desired impact

Think about the kind of impact you want to have on the world or your community. Ask yourself how you would like to be remembered and what legacy you wish to leave behind.

Step Five: Craft your purpose statement

Begin with a draft where you freely write your thoughts on how your values and passions translate into your purpose. Try to encapsulate your purpose in a clear, concise statement. It should ideally be one or two sentences.

Step Six: Review and refine

Reflect on your draft and refine it. Your purpose statement should feel authentic and inspiring to you. It should encapsulate what you believe to be your role or contribution to the world.

Step Seven: Visualization

Visualize yourself living out your purpose. How does it feel? What are you doing differently?

Step Eight: Seek feedback

If it feels comfortable, share your purpose statement with a trusted friend or family member for feedback. Sometimes, external perspectives can provide valuable insights.

Step Nine: Living Your purpose statement

Once you have your purpose statement, think about ways you can live out this purpose in your daily life. Consider your current actions and decisions and how they align with this statement.

Step Ten: Review and evolve

Remember that your purpose statement can evolve over time. Revisit and revise it as you grow, and your life circumstances change.

This exercise is a powerful tool for bringing clarity and focus to your life. A well-articulated purpose statement can serve as a guiding light, helping you make decisions that are aligned with your deepest values and aspirations. It's about defining your path and ensuring that your actions are in harmony with your true self.

Case Studies and Real-Life Examples

Let's explore some fresh examples of individuals who discovered their purpose and how it transformed their lives, focusing on different fields and backgrounds.

Harriet Tubman, Abolitionist and Underground Railroad Conductor

Purpose Discovery

Harriet Tubman discovered her purpose in fighting for the freedom of enslaved people. Born into slavery, she escaped and then made it her mission to help others gain their freedom. Tubman's commitment to this cause was fueled by her own experiences of brutality and oppression, as well as her deep religious faith.

Transformation

Tubman's discovery of her purpose transformed her life from that of an escaped slave to a leading abolitionist. She became one of the most famous "conductors" of the Underground Railroad, leading over 70 enslaved people to freedom across 13 missions. Her unwavering dedication and fearless actions not only saved lives but also made her a symbol of courage and resistance against the institution of slavery. Tubman's legacy continues to inspire generations in the fight for justice and equality.

Chef Massimo Bottura, Combating food waste

Purpose Discovery
Massimo Bottura, an Italian chef, is renowned for his innovative culinary practices. Bottura found his purpose in addressing food waste and hunger, far beyond the confines of traditional culinary arts.

Transformation
He opened community kitchens around the world, transforming surplus food from supermarkets and local suppliers into meals for the needy. His purpose-driven initiative has brought attention to food waste and hunger, blending culinary art with social activism.

Patricia Bath, Pioneering ophthalmologist

Purpose Discovery
Dr. Patricia Bath, an African American ophthalmologist, faced gender and racial barriers in her medical career. Her purpose was rooted in her passion for helping others see, leading her to focus on ophthalmology and community eye health, especially for underserved populations.

Transformation
She invented the Laserphaco Probe™ for cataract treatment and became the first African American woman to receive a medical patent. Her work significantly advanced the field of ophthalmology and made eye care more accessible to those who previously had limited access.

Greta Thunberg, Environmental activist

Purpose Discovery

Greta Thunberg, a Swedish teenager, began her activism journey with a solitary school strike for climate change. Greta found her purpose in advocating for urgent action to combat climate change, driven by a deep concern for the planet.

Transformation

Her activism sparked a global movement, inspiring millions of young people to join her in calling for environmental action. Her determination has significantly impacted global discussions on climate change policies.

These examples showcase how discovering and embracing one's purpose can lead to profound personal transformation and significant societal impact. Each of these individuals shifted from personal or localized experiences to broader, purpose-driven initiatives that have left lasting imprints in their respective fields.

Work out your own Purpose

To help you reflect on your own purpose, here are some practical exercises and reflective questions designed to facilitate self-discovery and clarity.

1. **Create a personal timeline**
   Create a timeline of your life, highlighting key moments, achievements, and challenges. Reflect on each event and ask, "What did this experience teach me about what I value most?"

2. **Make a vision board**
   Make a vision board that represents your aspirations and what brings you joy and fulfillment. Use images, words, or symbols to represent your dreams and goals.

3. **React to these journaling prompts**

   Take your journal—if you don't keep a journal, choose a simple blank notebook, and grab a pen—and brainstorm answers to these questions. (Pro tip: Slip your notebook into your pocket so that you can keep working on these answers in odd moments.)

   - "When do I feel most fulfilled and happy?"
   - "What activities make me lose track of time?"
   - "Which accomplishments am I most proud of and why?"

4. **Ask yourself, "Why?" five times**

   Think about a goal or activity you're engaged in. Ask yourself, "Why am I doing this?"

Write down your answer. Looking at your answer, ask yourself again, "Why...?" For example, "Why do I enjoy my job?" Answer: "Because it brings me money."

Keep asking *why?* In this example, you might ask, "Why is it important to me to bring in money?" Answer: "Because..."

Continue to challenge your answers so that you ask yourself five times, *Why?* This will help you drill down to your root purpose and can uncover some surprising insights that weren't obvious to you at first.

1. **Meditation and mindfulness**

   Practice mindfulness or meditation, focusing on your thoughts and feelings about your life's direction. Afterward, reflect on any insights or recurring themes that emerge.

2. **Talk to your close ones**

   Ask friends, family, or colleagues about when they've seen you most engaged and enthusiastic. Discuss their observations and how they align with your perceptions.

3. **Assess your skills and talents**

   List out your skills and talents. Reflect on how you can use them to impact others or contribute to something meaningful. Ask, "Which of my skills do I enjoy using the most and why?"

4. **What's your ideal day?**

   Describe in detail your ideal day from morning to night in a world where there are no constraints. Analyze this description to uncover what aspects are most important to you.

5. **Reflect on legacy**

   Consider the question, "What would I want to be remembered for?" Think about how this aligns with your current life path and choices.

6. **Explore your values**

   Make a list of your core values. Reflect on how your current life aligns with these values. Identify any gaps and consider changes that would bring your life more in line with these values.

These exercises and questions are designed to spark introspection and guide you towards a clearer understanding of your own purpose. They help uncover your passions, values, and strengths, forming the foundation upon which your purpose-driven life can be built. Now take the following steps to consolidate your understanding of your purpose.

- Write down your understanding of the term "purpose"
- Reflect on how your own purpose has influenced your life decisions
- Explore methods to discover your personal purpose
- Share your thoughts on how having a clear purpose can align with your Black Dot goals.

The Role of Discipline

In this section, we are going to look at what discipline is and why you should want to cultivate it. Then, we'll look at a few famous people and how they achieved their purpose and overcame their Black Dots through exercising discipline, and finally we will take a look at how you can cultivate better discipline.

So, what is discipline?

The elements of discipline

I define discipline as the ability to control one's impulses and to balance emotion against reason; to focus on tasks, along with adopting a structured approach to the things you need to do; and to persevere through challenges.

Let's take a close look at each of those elements that, taken together, make for a disciplined approach.

Control of impulses

Self-control is fundamental to the practice of discipline. Discipline involves the ability to control one's impulses, desires, and wishes for immediate gratification. Self-control happens when you make choices that align with long-term goals rather than succumb to short-term temptations.

To be able to exercise self-control, you need to be able to prioritize long-term benefits over your immediate pleasure. This aspect of discipline is crucial for success in any endeavor.

Discipline also involves managing one's emotional responses. It's about not letting frustration, fatigue, or other emotions derail your efforts. A disciplined mindset enables more rational and thoughtful decision-making, as opposed to decisions driven by fleeting emotions or impulses.

Focus on tasks

Discipline enables you to focus your attention on the task at hand. It's about maintaining concentration and not allowing distractions to divert your efforts away from your goals. A disciplined approach ensures that once you begin a task, you see it through to completion. It's about following through on your commitments and responsibilities.

Discipline involves a structured approach to tasks and goals. It includes planning, organizing, and executing tasks in a systematic manner. Over time, discipline leads to the development of productive habits that can automate certain behaviors, making it easier to maintain a disciplined approach.

Persevering through challenges

Discipline is closely linked to Resilience—the ability to persist even when beset by difficulties and setbacks. Disciplined individuals don't give up easily when faced with obstacles. Perseverance, a key component of discipline, involves applying consistent effort towards a goal, even when progress seems slow, or challenges arise.

To sum up, discipline is a multifaceted concept and a key determinant of success and personal growth. Exercise discipline and you will enable yourself to achieve your goals and realize your full potential.

Discipline is a skill that can be learned

Even if you are secretly thinking, "Jerry, I have no self-discipline," take heart. Discipline is not a fixed trait, an innate characteristic that some people are born with, and others are not, but a skill that can be developed and strengthened over time.

Start with small, manageable tasks and progressively increase their complexity, or duration, and you will find you can build discipline over time.

Discipline begins with establishing routines and habits. By consistently following a routine, even a simple one, you can train yourself to be more disciplined. As the habits you've adopted become ingrained, the need for conscious self-control decreases because your disciplined behaviors are becoming automatic.

You can train your mind and emotions to become more disciplined. There are exercises that strengthen willpower, such as helping you to resist temptation or delay gratification. Engaging in mindfulness and meditation can improve your self-awareness and emotional regulation, which are key components of discipline.

Create an environment that supports disciplined behavior. This might involve removing distractions or setting up specific spaces for focused work.

Find someone to hold you accountable for building your discipline, whether a mentor, a coach, or a peer.

If you experience setbacks, viewing them as learning opportunities rather than failures. Each challenge is an opportunity to improve and strengthen your discipline. It is vital to understand this so that you do not become disheartened and give up.

Being disciplined is not a rigid state; it also involves being adaptable. Practice the ability to adjust and refine strategies as you learn what works best for you.

Use the technique of positive reinforcement to reinforce disciplined behavior. When you recognize and celebrate small victories, you are encouraging yourself to continue to strengthen your self-discipline.

Discipline is a skill that anyone can develop with intentional effort and practice. It involves building and maintaining habits, training yourself in mental and emotional control, creating supportive environments, continuously learning and adapting, and using positive reinforcement. Understand discipline as a dynamic skill that you can develop, and you've opened up the possibility of significant personal growth and achievement.

The psychology of discipline

Let's delve into the psychological principles that underpin discipline so that I can give you deeper insight into how discipline works. When you know how it works, you can cultivate it more effectively.

Delayed Gratification

The famous Marshmallow Test conducted by psychologist Walter Mischel plays a pivotal role in understanding delayed gratification. It showed that children who could resist the temptation of an immediate reward (a marshmallow) in favor of a promised, larger reward later tended to have better life outcomes.

Delayed gratification involves the ability to prioritize long-term benefits over immediate pleasures. This future-oriented mindset is a cornerstone of disciplined behavior that impacts decision-making and the pursuit of your goals.

Willpower and Self-Control

Willpower is sometimes likened to a muscle that can be strengthened over time through use. Engaging in tasks that require self-control can enhance one's capacity for discipline.

However, there is a caveat. Another argument runs that willpower can be depleted with over-use. Therefore, it's important to manage it wisely and create automatic habits that reduce the constant need to exercise self-control through willpower.

Habit Formation

Habit formation is key to discipline. By turning disciplined actions into habits, the need for the effort of maintaining constant willpower is reduced as these actions become more automatic.

Understanding the habit loop (cue-routine-reward) can help in creating and maintaining disciplined habits.

Planning and decision-making

Discipline is closely linked to executive functions in the brain, which include planning, decision-making, and impulse control. Strengthening these functions can enhance discipline.

The brain's ability to change and adapt (neuroplasticity) means that engaging in disciplined behavior can physically strengthen these neural pathways over time.

Motivation and discipline

It's important to understand the difference between intrinsic (internal) and extrinsic (external) motivation. While extrinsic motivators, reasons for doing something that lie wholly outside yourself, can be effective, intrinsic motivators are stronger. This is because when actions are aligned with your own personal values (an intrinsic motivator), discipline becomes more natural and less of a struggle. This is when you will find it easier to sustain disciplined behavior.

Cognitive strategies

Cognitive strategies like reframing thoughts and adopting a growth mindset can enhance one's ability to be disciplined. For example, view challenges as opportunities for growth rather than obstacles.

Emotional regulation

Discipline involves the ability to manage your emotions effectively, particularly in stressful or tempting situations. Techniques such as mindfulness can help you to regulate your emotions.

You see how powerful knowledge can be? Now you know how discipline works inside your head, it will be easier to develop disciplined behaviors that increase your personal effectiveness and achievement. But before we look at the practicalities of developing disciplined behaviors, let's take a moment to look at the impact of discipline on your life.

The impact of discipline

The exercise of discipline significantly affects both your behavior and your decision-making. It influences how we act, respond to challenges, and make choices in our daily lives.

Influences daily behavior

When you exercise discipline, you will foster consistency in your behavior. You will find it easier to stick to your routines and commitments, even when faced with distractions or temptations.

Discipline encourages habit formation. Over time, your disciplined actions become habits. These habits then shape your daily behavior and make it easier to maintain a disciplined approach without relying heavily on willpower.

Improves decision-making

Discipline helps you to make more rational and thought-out decisions. You will be able to resist making impulsive choices that might feel gratifying in the short term but are detrimental in the long term.

When you are disciplined, you are more likely to make decisions that align with your long-term goals and values. This alignment ensures that your choices consistently contribute to your overarching objectives.

Enhances self-control

One of the key aspects of discipline is the ability to manage impulses. This control is crucial in situations that require patience, endurance, or adherence to a plan, such as in academic or professional settings.

Your impulse may be to seek an immediate reward. Discipline strengthens your capacity to delay gratification. You will find it easier to forego immediate pleasure in favor of greater, long-term rewards. This is a critical aspect of successful decision-making.

Makes you resilient

Discipline equips you to remain steadfast in your pursuits even when faced with obstacles or setbacks. This resilience influences your behavior in challenging situations and promotes perseverance.

When you encounter difficulties, as a disciplined individual you are more likely to make adaptive decisions that help you stay on course towards your goals.

Gives you a long-term perspective

Discipline helps you to maintain your focus on future outcomes. This long-term perspective is vital for making decisions that contribute to your future success and fulfillment.

As part of that focus on future outcomes, disciplined behavior supports strategic planning. Disciplined behavior influences your decision-making by encouraging you to adopt a more calculated and foresighted approach to achieving your objectives.

Emotional regulation

Discipline helps you to regulate your emotional responses, ensuring that your decisions are not overly influenced by fleeting emotions like anger, frustration, or excitement. By managing your emotions effectively, you will be able to make more mindful and balanced choices.

So, you see how discipline profoundly impacts your behavior and decision-making? It instills in you a sense of consistency and control. It enables you to exercise strategic foresight in your actions and choices, aligning them with your personal goals and values. This disciplined approach leads to more effective and successful outcomes.

Discipline and your goals

Discipline acts as a crucial bridge between *setting* goals and *accomplishing* them. To put it another way, discipline bridges the gap between your long-term aspirations and short-term actions. It ensures that your daily efforts contribute to the achievement of bigger, long-term objectives.

When you use discipline to accomplish your goals, it is enabling you to tackle the Black Dots in your life, and so to realize your full potential.

Let's delve deeper into the connection between being disciplined and achieving meaningful goals so that you can see for yourself why it is so important to exercise self-discipline.

Discipline is the key to consistency

Think of discipline as the foundation for Action. To progress, you must be consistent. If you want to make continuous progress towards your goals, then you need to turn up consistently to do what you need to reach your goals.

Discipline is what drives your consistent effort towards your goals, regardless of obstacles or how you feel on any given day. It's about doing what needs to be done, even when it's not easy or convenient.

Discipline challenges procrastination

Discipline helps you to overcome any tendency you have towards procrastination and to stay focused on tasks despite distractions that might derail your progress.

It's natural to procrastinate when we are trying to achieve goals we perceive as difficult, tedious, or even painful. Procrastination creates a barrier between ourselves and our goals but discipline helps to break through the barrier.

By cultivating a disciplined approach, you're more likely to tackle tasks promptly, which is crucial for achieving significant accomplishments.

Form habits to sustain discipline

Once you understand the importance of cultivating discipline, you need to form and sustain habits. The development of daily habits and routines ensures that you are regularly working towards your goals.

It is important to start small and gradually increase the complexity or intensity of the tasks you have identified to reach your goals. This approach helps you to build discipline without overwhelming yourself.

Later in this section, I will show you how to create routines, set reminders, and establish a conducive environment for building and sustaining your practice of discipline.

Cultivating healthy habits

Discipline extends to personal habits, including health and wellness. Maintaining a healthy lifestyle through disciplined habits like regular exercise, proper diet, and sufficient rest is essential for keeping your mind and body in optimal condition to achieve your potential.

Discipline enhances efficiency

It allows you to concentrate your energy and resources on your most important goals, avoiding distractions. This focused approach ensures that your efforts are maximized, bringing you closer to realizing your full potential.

Discipline also affects the quality of your work. It encourages thoroughness, attention to detail, and a commitment to excellence. These are all important for achieving high standards in any endeavor.

Discipline enhances your growth

Effective discipline not only enables you to manage your time efficiently, by helping you to align your actions with goals, but it also has a much more profound, longer-term impact on you. When you ensure that your everyday actions are goal-oriented, discipline helps you to gradually realize your potential. You'll systematically work on developing your skills and talents, thereby unlocking your full abilities.

SUMMARY

Whether you are learning a new skill, or working on a project, or pursuing personal improvement, consistent action is essential. Discipline ensures that you make steady progress toward your goals, even in small increments.

Discipline fosters resilience

When you have a long course of action to follow to reach your goal, your emotions are going to take a beating when you are faced with setbacks, or even just because your progress feels slow. Discipline is closely linked to resilience—the ability to bounce back from setbacks.

A disciplined mindset prepares you to face challenges and obstacles more effectively, learning from them and persisting despite difficulties. Discipline helps you to maintain your path towards your goals. It helps you to manage your emotions effectively, particularly in moments of frustration or demotivation.

Discipline aids accountability

If you are to deal with your Black Dots effectively, being disciplined will help you to track your progress and be accountable for the daily actions you have decided to carry out. This might involve keeping a journal, using apps, or having an accountability partner.

As you move along the path to achieving your goals, you may need to adjust your strategies for dealing with your Black Dots. That means you will need to reassess your position in a disciplined way and to adjust your strategies so that your actions remain aligned with your goals.

Discipline in decision-making

Though it may not be immediately obvious, discipline plays a role in thoughtful decision-making. Discipline helps you to maintain a long-term vision, and to make choices that are aligned with your long-term goals, not ones that only bring you immediate gratification.

In essence, discipline is not just about rigid control or willpower; it's a powerful tool to use to unlock and realize your potential. It's about creating a structured approach to your life and goals. It ensures that your efforts are consistent, focused, and aligned with your objectives. Over time, that enables you to fully realize your potential. This disciplined approach is what transforms *aspirations* into tangible *achievements* and is fundamental to personal and professional success.

People who have transformed their lives by discipline

Let's explore some real-life stories of individuals who have significantly transformed their lives through the power of discipline. These examples illustrate how discipline can lead to remarkable personal and professional achievements:

J.K. Rowling—From struggling writer to bestselling author

Before her success, J.K. Rowling faced numerous challenges, including living as a single mother on welfare and coping with depression.

Discipline in action

Rowling wrote the first "Harry Potter" book in various cafes while caring for her daughter. Despite numerous rejections from publishers, she continued to write and revise her manuscript.

Transformation

Her discipline and perseverance paid off, leading to the publication of the "Harry Potter" series, which became a global phenomenon that transformed her life and the lives of millions of readers.

Howard Schultz—Building Starbucks into a global brand

Howard Schultz, the former CEO of Starbucks, grew up in a poor housing complex in Brooklyn.

Discipline in action

Schultz's discipline was evident in his commitment to his vision for Starbucks. He worked tirelessly to expand the company, often working long hours, and persistently pushing for the high standards he envisioned.

Transformation

His disciplined approach to business and leadership transformed Starbucks into one of the world's most recognizable and successful coffee brands.

Oprah Winfrey—Media mogul and philanthropist

Oprah Winfrey overcame a difficult childhood marked by poverty and abuse to become a media mogul.

Discipline in action

Oprah's discipline was key in her career, from honing her skills as a talk show host to managing her business ventures and philanthropic activities.

Transformation

Her disciplined work ethic and persistence led to the creation of a media empire and made her a role model and influential figure worldwide.

Elon Musk—Innovator and entrepreneur

Known for his work with Tesla, SpaceX, and other ventures, Musk is recognized for his ambitious and challenging projects.

Discipline in action

Musk's disciplined approach to his work is evident in his hands-on involvement in multiple groundbreaking projects simultaneously, often pushing the boundaries of innovation.

Transformation

His discipline in pursuing innovative and challenging projects has not only transformed his life but has also had a significant impact on various industries, from automotive to space exploration.

Michael Phelps—Most decorated Olympian

American swimmer Michael Phelps is the most decorated Olympian of all time.

Discipline in action

Phelps's training regimen was famously intense, involving hours of swimming, dryland workouts, careful diet, and recovery routines.

Transformation

His disciplined approach to training and competition led to a record-breaking 28 Olympic medals, transforming him into an icon in the world of sports.

Each of these people show, through their lived experience, the transformative power of discipline. Whether in the realm of literature, business, media, innovation, or sports, they are proof that disciplined effort and unwavering commitment to their goals can lead to extraordinary achievements and life transformations.

Why discipline is so closely linked to success

The idea that disciplined individuals are more likely to succeed in their endeavors is a key concept in understanding the role of discipline in achieving personal and professional goals.

Discipline is closely linked to success for these reasons:

Consistency in efforts

Disciplined individuals are consistent in their efforts toward their goals. They understand that regular progress, even if small, is crucial in achieving long-term objectives. They also understand that discipline leads to the formation of productive habits which, over time, become ingrained and easier to maintain.

Effective time management

Discipline involves effective time management, allowing individuals to prioritize tasks that align with their goals, ensuring that their time is used efficiently. A disciplined approach helps in avoiding procrastination, ensuring that important tasks are not left until the last minute.

Goal-oriented focus

Disciplined individuals can maintain focus on their goals, avoiding distractions that can derail their plans. They make sure that their daily actions are in alignment with their overarching objectives, which is essential for success.

Resilience in the face of challenges

Discipline fosters resilience, enabling individuals to face challenges and setbacks without veering off course. Disciplined individuals are more likely to adapt their strategies in response to changing circumstances. This is critical for success in dynamic environments.

Continuous improvement

Discipline encourages a mindset of continuous learning and growth. Disciplined individuals are more likely to seek out opportunities for self-improvement, which contributes to their success. They are also more open to feedback and are more willing to adjust their approach as needed. Both qualities are crucial for personal and professional development.

Achieving long-term goals

Disciplined individuals are better equipped to keep their long-term vision in focus, ensuring that short-term actions contribute to their ultimate goals. The cumulative effect of disciplined daily actions significantly increases the likelihood of achieving long-term success.

SUMMARY

Discipline is a key determinant of success. It's about more than just willpower; it's a systematic approach to life that encompasses consistent efforts, effective time management, goal-oriented focus, resilience, continuous improvement, and a long-term perspective. These attributes of disciplined individuals significantly enhance their chances of success in various endeavors.

How to Cultivate Discipline

Cultivating discipline is a key aspect of achieving personal and professional success. It involves developing a set of habits and mindsets that encourage consistency and perseverance in the attainment of your goals.

Let's look at some practical strategies for cultivating discipline in everyday life. These strategies are designed to help you to establish routines, set boundaries, and enhance self-control.

Set clear goals

Discipline begins with having a clear understanding of what you want to achieve. Set specific, measurable, and achievable goals. Ensure these goals align with your values and larger life objectives and use the SMART framework (more on goal-setting, later.) When your goals are clear, it's easier to stay focused and disciplined in pursuing them.

Develop routines

Establishing routines is crucial for building discipline. Create daily or weekly routines that align with your goals. Consistency in these routines helps in reinforcing discipline as a habit. Stick to your routine as closely as possible, even on days when motivation is low.

Begin by establishing small routines that you can maintain. This could be as simple as a morning routine or dedicating a specific time each day for a particular task. As small routines become habitual, gradually add more complex or challenging elements to them.

Make sure to clearly define the times you want to work and the times you want to relax. This helps in maintaining a balance and prevents burnout.

Break tasks into smaller steps

Large tasks can be overwhelming. Break them into smaller, manageable steps. This makes it easier to start and maintain momentum, which is essential for discipline.

Prioritize tasks

Learn to prioritize tasks based on their importance and urgency. Focus on high-priority tasks that align closely with your goals, and don't get sidetracked by less important activities.

Remove temptations and distractions

Identify and eliminate distractions that can derail your focus. Organize your workspace to minimize distractions and make it conducive to focused work. Turn off your phone and laptop's notifications. Set specific times for checking your emails. Utilize tools and apps that help you to maintain focus and minimize interruptions.

Practice self-control

Discipline requires self-control. Practice making decisions that align with your long-term goals, even if they require sacrificing short-term pleasures. Practice your ability to delay gratification in small ways, like waiting a bit longer for a break, or resisting an impulse purchase. Make sure you get adequate rest and relaxation because willpower can be depleted by stress and fatigue.

Mindfulness and meditation

Practices such as mindfulness and meditation can enhance self-awareness, which is vital for discipline. They help in understanding your habits and triggers, allowing you to make more disciplined choices. Incorporate mindfulness techniques into your daily life to increase your awareness of impulsive behaviors and learn to pause before acting on them.

Use positive reinforcement

Reward yourself for sticking to your disciplined plan. This positive reinforcement can motivate you to continue being disciplined.

Track your progress and stay accountable

Hold yourself accountable for your actions and progress. You can do this through self-reflection, keeping a journal, or having an accountability partner. Cultivate a social circle that values and practices discipline. Having supportive and like-minded individuals around you can be highly motivating.

Regularly reflect on your discipline practices. Assess what's working and what's not. Be willing to adapt and modify your strategies. Discipline is not about rigid adherence to rules but about finding what works best for you.

Learn from setbacks

Finally, view setbacks as learning opportunities. Discipline is not about being perfect; it's about learning from mistakes and continuing to move forward.

Cultivating discipline is a journey in which you develop habits, mindsets, and strategies that align with your goals. It's about making consistent efforts, even while you are coping with challenges and distractions, so that you maintain your focus on your ultimate objectives.

How to build your own practice of discipline

This exercise will identify the areas in which you need to exert discipline and will help you to implement small, manageable changes for improvement.

Follow these actionable steps to enhance your practice of discipline in your daily life.

Identify areas for discipline

Begin with a self-assessment to identify areas in your life where your practice of discipline could be improved. This could be in personal habits, work, studies, health, finances, or relationships.

Pinpoint your specific challenges within these areas. For instance, if the broader area is health, a specific challenge might be irregular exercise routines or unhealthy eating habits.

Set specific goals

For each challenge you identify, set specific, achievable goals. Use the SMART criteria (Specific, Measurable, Achievable, Relevant, and Time-bound) to ensure these goals are well-defined and realistic.

Write down these goals. Writing them increases your sense of commitment and clarity.

Implement small changes

Break down your goals into small, manageable steps. For example, if your goal is to exercise regularly, start with short, ten-minute workouts. These small steps will build momentum incrementally.

Incorporate these small steps into your daily routine. Consistency is key to building discipline.

Create a supportive environment

Modify your environment to support your disciplined behavior. Remove temptations or distractions that might hinder your progress.

Utilize tools, apps, or resources that can help you stay on track. This might include calendars, reminder apps, or accountability partners.

Monitor progress

Keep a log of your daily actions related to your Discipline goals. This could be a journal, spreadsheet, or app.

Set a regular time to review your progress. Reflect on what's working and what's not and adjust your approach accordingly.

Reward success

Recognize a milestone, no matter how small, and celebrate it when you reach it. This positive reinforcement motivates you to maintain your discipline.

Build resilience

Understand that setbacks are not failure, they are part of the process. Prepare strategies for dealing with them, such as motivational reminders or seeking support from friends or mentors.

Be flexible in your approach. If a certain method is not working, be willing to try different strategies.

Reflect and adjust

Regularly reflect on your experiences. What lessons have you learned? How have these small changes impacted your life?

Use these reflections to continuously improve and refine your approach to building discipline.

If you follow this step-by-step approach, you will enhance your practice of discipline. Note how important it is to make small changes, undertake a regular review, and adapt your practice for sustained improvement.

What you are doing here by practicing discipline is to slowly form habits. Next, we are going to look more closely at habits.

Formation of habits

Let's lean into the crucial role that habits play in maintaining discipline and achieving long-term goals. Habits are essentially behaviors that have become automatic through repetition. When a behavior becomes a habit, it requires less conscious effort and willpower to perform. This automatic behavior is key to maintaining discipline, as it reduces the mental load of making decisions about routine actions.

The formation of habits ensures you will be consistent in your actions, which is essential for disciplined behavior. Regular habits align with your goals and in turn, that ensures you are consistently working towards them.

Think of long-term goals as building blocks. You are going to take small steps to achieve your big goals. Achieving long-term goals is about consistently taking small, manageable steps. These steps, when turned into habits, become integrated into your daily life, steadily moving you towards your goals. The cumulative effect of daily habits can be profound. Over time, these small actions add up, significantly contributing to the achievement of larger, long-term objectives.

I cannot over-emphasize the importance of making small changes and of not trying to do too much all at once. Making small, incremental changes to your routines can be more effective than attempting major overhauls, which can be overwhelming and unsustainable. Consistent small actions lay a foundation upon which more complex habits can be built. As the habit becomes ingrained, you can gradually increase the complexity or duration of the behavior.

Small changes are less intimidating and more manageable, making it easier to start and stick with new habits. For example, beginning with just 15–20 minutes of exercise a day is more feasible than an hour for someone new to fitness. Over time, these small changes can have a compound effect. Just as small financial savings can grow into substantial amounts over time, small habitual changes can lead to significant transformations.

Habits, by nature, are repetitive. It is important to understand that habits are formed through a loop process that is made up of three parts. The first part is a cue that triggers a routine. The second part is the routine in which you perform an action, or a series of them. The third part is the reward that results from the routine.

For example, the habit of brushing your teeth in the morning might be triggered by finishing breakfast. Finishing breakfast is your cue. The cue triggers the routine: the act of brushing your teeth. Completion of the routine results in a reward: the good sensation of cleanliness.

From a neurological perspective, as this loop is repeated over time, the brain begins to automate the behavior, making it require less conscious effort.

Recognizing the cues that trigger routines and the rewards that reinforce them is crucial in habit formation. Once you understand what the cues, triggers, and rewards are for a particular habit, you can alter the habit by either modifying them or forming a new habit to replace it. For example, changing your environment can alter cues, and introducing new rewards can reinforce desired routines.

To form productive habits, identify behaviors that directly contribute to your goals. For example, if your goal is to write a book, a key habit might be *to write for a set period* each day.

Integrate these behaviors into your daily routine. Consistency, in timing and context, is key to helping you solidify new habits. It's more effective to engage in a small behavior regularly than to do a lot irregularly.

Make it easy for yourself to carry out your new habits. Set up physical reminders or arrange your space to make the desired action easier. Removing obstacles that make it hard to perform the habit is as important: This could be as simple as keeping your running shoes next to your bed if you want to develop a habit of morning jogging. Be prepared to make adjustments. What works initially might need tweaking as you progress.

Of course, you aren't working with a completely blank canvas here. Forgive me for saying so, but you may have a few bad habits that need to be overcome if you want to maintain your disciplined practice in sustaining good habits. They key to overcoming bad habits is to be aware of them, first of all, and then actively work to replace them with positive ones.

As ever when you are engaging in a process, it is important to keep track of your habits and monitor your process. Use a journal or an app, or whatever suits you best, but make sure you keep yourself accountable and reinforce the process of forming good habits. But remember, habit formation takes time and persistence. It's important to be patient and not get discouraged if your progress seems slow.

Make sure you acknowledge and celebrate those milestones along the way. Immediate rewards can reinforce the habit loop. These rewards don't have to be big; they can be as simple as the satisfaction of ticking off a task on your to-do list. The satisfaction you feel, the positive feelings you experience when you complete a small task, is an important part of the cycle. It reinforces the habit and motivates you, making it more likely you'll repeat it, and it validates your practice of discipline.

The Importance of Goals

Let's take a moment to review why setting goals matters. Understanding the psychological aspects enhances the effectiveness of goal-setting strategies in both your personal and professional domains.

- You achieve clarity and focus in your day-to-day actions
- You can measure your progress towards a goal
- You can transform your challenges into achievable goals
- You gain increased motivation to achieve your goals
- Your sense of self-efficacy can flourish.

Clarity and focus

Goals provide clarity and focus. They turn abstract aspirations into concrete targets. Setting specific, measurable, and achievable goals is a key tenet of the Black Dot Philosophy.

Measuring progress

Goals allow for the measurement of progress. They offer milestones that you can work towards, so you can constantly assess your progress, and in turn that helps you to maintain your motivation and a sense of achievement. This feedback is crucial for motivation as it allows you to see how close you are to achieving your goal. If you are struggling, it gives you the data you need to change your strategy.

Transformation of challenges

You are going to be dealing with your Black Dots and that means you need an actionable plan to transform them into goals that you can achieve. By converting your Black Dots (challenges) into Goals, you shift your perspective from seeing obstacles as blocks, or setbacks, to seeing them as opportunities for growth.

Increased motivation

Goals provide a sense of direction and focus. When you set a goal, you have a clear end-point or target to aim for. This direction helps you to channel your energy and effort towards specific activities, enhancing your focus and reducing wasted effort. It is important to get the balance right, between challenge and achievability. Goals that are too easy may not provide enough challenge to motivate, while overly ambitious goals can lead to frustration and demotivation.

According to psychological theories such as those set out in the book *Goal-Setting Theory* by Locke and Latham, a challenging goal leads to higher performance as long as you see the goal as attainable. The effort to achieve these goals can be motivating in itself.

From a neurological perspective, achieving a goal can trigger the release of dopamine, a neurotransmitter associated with feelings of pleasure and satisfaction. This release can create a positive association with goal-directed behavior, reinforcing the motivation to pursue and achieve goals.

Goal-setting can tap into both intrinsic (internal) motivation, such as personal growth or enjoyment, and extrinsic (external) motivation, like rewards or recognition. Balancing these motivations is important, as intrinsic motivation is often more sustainable in the long run.

Try visualizing yourself achieving your goals. It can be a powerful motivator. By imagining the successful outcome, you can foster a stronger connection and commitment to your goals.

Publicly declaring your goals can increase your commitment to achieving them. You may find the psychological pressure of social expectation serves as an additional motivator.

Self-efficacy

Achieving goals, especially challenging ones, can boost self-efficacy—the belief in your own ability to succeed. This increased confidence can create a positive feedback loop, where success breeds more success and motivation.

How to set your goals

SMART goals are a fundamental tool in the Black Dot Philosophy. They provide a systematic and effective approach to goal-setting in a way that will help you to overcome your Black Dots.

It is important to know exactly what you are aiming for when you set a goal. That is why we talk about setting SMART goals, that is, goals that are Specific, Measurable, Achievable, Relevant, and Time-bound.

Specific goals provide clear direction with no ambiguity about what is to be achieved. This specificity eliminates ambiguity, making it easier to focus your efforts and resources effectively. Write down your goals—don't just think about them—so that you make your goals as specific as possible. Clearly define what you want to achieve, including the who, what, where, when, and why. That is how you turn abstract aspirations into tangible targets.

Measurable goals allow for the tracking of progress. When goals are quantifiable, it is easier to assess how far you have come, how much further you need to go and whether you need to make any adjustments along the way. Measurement can be a strong motivator. To ensure your goals are measurable, answer the question, "How shall I measure this?" Then, establish concrete criteria for measuring your progress and success.

Setting Achievable goals ensures that they are realistic and within reach. While goals should be challenging, they also need to be attainable with the resources and time you have. Keep them in the realm of possibility. This balance is crucial to maintain motivation and prevent discouragement.

Relevant goals align with your broader life objectives and values. We will say more about aligning your goals to your purpose shortly. This alignment ensures that the effort put into achieving these goals contributes meaningfully to overall life plans and personal growth.

Goals need to be Time-bound. Having a time-frame provides a sense of urgency and a deadline that helps to maintain focus and momentum. Time-bound goals encourage you to prioritize tasks, manage your time effectively, and make consistent progress. So, set a deadline for your goals. When are you going to reach it?

By adhering to the SMART criteria, goals become more than just wishes or aspirations; they transform into concrete targets with a clear plan of action. Adopting this structure is essential for navigating the journey towards achieving your goal, especially in the context of addressing and overcoming the Black Dots in your life.

Clear goals provide direction and focus. They help in prioritizing actions and resources, ensuring that efforts are concentrated on what matters most. Clarity helps you to make good decisions, as you can evaluate your choices based on whether they align with or detract from your goals.

Effective goal-setting is not just about identifying what you want to achieve; it's also about strategically planning and consistently working towards these goals. The strategies I'm about to tell you to adopt are probably starting to sound familiar, and the reason for that is you are learning to build good habits and practice discipline in service of overcoming your Black Dots.

This is what you need to do. Spend time visualizing what it will be like to have successfully achieved your goals. Visualizing the outcome can boost motivation and commitment because it creates an emotional connection to the goal.

If you have multiple goals, prioritize them. Focus on the goals that are most important to you, and will have the greatest impact, first.

For each goal, develop a detailed action plan. Outline the steps you need to take, resources required, potential obstacles, and strategies for overcoming them.

Don't hesitate to seek feedback and support from mentors, peers, or professionals. External perspectives can provide valuable insights and encouragement.

Celebrate the small victories and milestones along the way. This recognition can provide motivation and a sense of accomplishment.

Regularly reflect on your goals and the progress you've made. Be open to adjusting your goals as you grow. You are likely to experience setbacks or discover new learnings—this is a normal part of the process of reaching for your goals. Flexibility is important, as circumstances and priorities can change.

Follow this advice and you will enhance your goal-setting process, making it more effective and aligned with your aspirations and capabilities.

The Connection between Discipline and Goals

We have looked at the importance of cultivating the practice of discipline so that we can carry out the actions that will address our Black Dots. We are going to consider, now, the intrinsic relationship between discipline and effective goal pursuit.

Think of discipline as the engine that propels your progress toward achieving meaningful goals. It's the driving force that keeps you moving forward, especially when your motivation wanes or obstacles arise.

The regular, consistent actions driven by discipline are crucial in transforming goals from something yet to be attained into reality.

Discipline fosters resilience, enabling you to persevere through challenges and setbacks that might otherwise derail your progress towards goals.

Disciplined individuals are better equipped to assess, learn from setbacks, and adjust their strategies accordingly.

Discipline helps you to keep your focus on long-term goals, even when you are faced with short-term distractions or challenges. It encourages you to prioritize daily tasks and actions that are aligned with your long-term objectives.

Discipline is crucial in the planning phase of goal pursuit, aiding in setting realistic, achievable goals and developing strategic plans to achieve them. It plays a vital role in the execution of these plans. When you are disciplined, you follow through your plans with consistent action.

You are probably finding that your goals require the formation of new habits, or the alteration of existing ones. Discipline helps you to be consistent in the practice necessary for habit formation. Over time, the disciplined practice of these habits leads to you perform them automatically, making goal-oriented actions easier and more natural.

Discipline is key to managing your time effectively, ensuring that your effort is focused on goal-relevant activities. It also involves the optimal allocation of other resources, such as energy and finances, towards goal attainment.

A disciplined approach includes regularly reviewing progress towards goals, assessing what is working and what is not. Discipline enables you to make responsive adjustments based on feedback, keeping you aligned with your goals.

Do you see how it is not just about having goals but also about the disciplined pursuit of these goals? Pursuing your goals involves sustained effort, resilience in overcoming challenges, and strategic planning and execution. It demands habit formation, effective time and resource management, and the ability to review and adjust course as necessary. That's why you need Discipline to reach your goals.

Now we are going to bring forward another theme we have already looked at, your purpose, and see why it is so important to align your goals with your purpose.

Goal-setting with Purpose

Goals should act as a tangible manifestation of your purpose. Remember that Purpose can be thought of as the overarching *why* behind your actions—your core reason for doing what you do. It's your fundamental motivation or the driving force behind your aspirations. Your purpose represents your core values, passions, and what you find most meaningful in life. It acts as a compass, guiding your choices and actions.

Living in alignment with your purpose typically leads to greater fulfillment, as your actions resonate with your deepest values and aspirations.

While purpose provides a broad sense of direction, it may be abstract. It embodies your values and visions but may lack specific actionable steps.

Goals translate the abstract concept of purpose into concrete objectives. They are the specific, tangible targets you set to realize your broader purpose. They should provide both a sense of direction and a concrete plan for realizing that purpose.

When you set goals that are aligned with your purpose, especially when your goals are to deal with the Black Dots in your life, you are on track to lead a meaningful and fulfilling life.

For example, someone whose purpose revolves around personal health and wellness might set goals that include regular exercise, healthy eating, and mindfulness practices. Their purpose provides the motivation to maintain these healthy habits, even when it's challenging.

A professional whose purpose is to make impactful contributions in their field, such as a researcher whose goal is to innovate in renewable energy, will set purpose-driven goals that guide their career path, research focus, and ongoing commitment to their field.

A student with a purpose of lifelong learning and personal growth might set goals to pursue higher education or learn new skills. Their purpose fuels their ongoing educational pursuits, even amid obstacles such as time constraints or financial challenges.

For someone driven by a purpose to serve their community, goals might involve volunteering, community organizing, or advocacy work. Their clear sense of purpose inspires them to engage in these activities consistently and meaningfully.

Goals give direction to your purpose. They outline what needs to be done to fulfill your overarching vision or mission. Setting goals aligned with your purpose ensures that your daily actions are coherent with your deeper intentions and values. This alignment ensures that your efforts and achievements are not just successful by external standards but are also relevant and meaningful to you personally.

This alignment leads to a more holistic approach to life, where your actions, goals, and purpose are in harmony, leading to greater personal fulfillment and effectiveness. Goals aligned with your purpose tap into intrinsic motivation, which is driven by internal rewards like personal growth and satisfaction. This intrinsic motivation typically leads to a higher level of engagement and commitment to your goals.

By setting goals, you operationalize your purpose. This means you create a clear pathway to bring your purpose to life through specific actions and milestones.

Beyond providing direction, goals also involve planning—determining the how, when, and what of achieving your purpose. This includes the strategies, resources, and timelines needed to reach your goals.

Goals break down the journey to fulfilling your purpose into trackable milestones. This allows you to measure progress, adjust strategies, and stay motivated.

As with every step of the journey to deal with your Black Dots, you will want regularly to reflect on your purpose so that you maintain alignment with your goals. It's important to check periodically if your goals still resonate with your purpose.

The process of working towards and achieving your goals provides a feedback loop, helping you refine your understanding of your purpose and how best to pursue it. Be open to adapting your goals as your understanding of your purpose evolves. As you grow and change, so might your interpretation of your purpose.

To sum up, goals give practical expression to one's purpose. They give you a clear direction, a structured plan, and measurable milestones for turning your abstract aspirations into reality. This alignment of purpose and goals ensures that each action you take is meaningful and directed towards fulfilling your true aspirations.

When goals and purpose are aligned, there's a sense of coherence in your life. Your actions, decisions, and goals all point in the same direction, creating a unified path forward and internal conflict is reduced as your daily actions and long-term goals are in harmony with your overarching purpose.

Define your own purpose-driven goals

Let me guide you through the process of identifying goals that deeply resonate with your purpose and encourage you to set both short-term and long-term goals.

Start by reflecting on your purpose. Consider what truly matters to you, what drives you, and what you are passionate about. Ask yourself what you want your legacy to be, or how you want to impact the world.

With your purpose in mind, brainstorm a list of potential goals. Don't limit yourself at this stage; write down all ideas that come to mind. Think about different areas of your life such as career, personal growth, health, relationships, and community.

Review your list of goals and evaluate how each aligns with your purpose. For each goal ask yourself, does it help advance your purpose or is merely a good idea? Select the goals that strongly resonate with your purpose and feel most meaningful to you.

Now take another look at your goals and put them into one of two groups: *Short-term goals* and *Long-term goals*.

Let's say that the short term is within the next year; the long term may be five years, ten years.

A goal that can be achieved in the short term should be a stepping stone that leads towards your larger purpose.

Long-term goals are typically more significant and closely tied to your overarching purpose.

Look at each goal and determine which group it falls into: Short-term, or Long-term.

Now let's look at each goal in more detail. Choose a goal and refine it, using the SMART criteria. Remember, SMART stands for Specific, Measurable, Achievable, Relevant, and Time-bound. Check that each goal measures up to these criteria. This step transforms vague aspirations into actionable goals. Repeat for each goal.

Having worked out goals that achieve your purpose, we can start to think now about how to go about achieving your goals. The first step is to create an Action Plan for each goal, detailing the steps you need to take to achieve it. In your plan, include notes on the resources you will need, identify potential obstacles, and jot down strategies to overcome them.

If your plan begins to feel overly complicated, it's a sign that the goal itself is large and complex. So, break down larger goals into smaller tasks to avoid feeling overwhelmed.

Establish a system for tracking your progress. This could involve regular check-ins, journaling, or using digital tools. Schedule periodic reviews of your goals to assess progress and make adjustments as needed.

Spend time visualizing the achievement of your goals. Imagine how fulfilling it will feel to accomplish goals aligned with your purpose. Use this visualization to stay motivated, especially when facing challenges.

Be open to modifying your goals as you grow and as your understanding of your purpose evolves. Flexibility is key to ensuring that your goals remain aligned with your purpose.

SUMMARY

When you define your purpose-driven goals, you are connecting your deepest motivations and aspirations to concrete objectives. It's worth repeating that by aligning your goals with your purpose, you ensure that your efforts lead to a fulfilling and meaningful life. This process encourages thoughtful consideration of what you truly want to achieve and gives you a structured approach to realizing those aspirations.

Tips to help prioritize your goals

Prioritizing and organizing your Black Dots and your goals is a vital step in effectively managing them. Here are some strategies that can be particularly helpful:

Categorize by life areas

Break down your challenges and goals into different areas of your life, such as personal, professional, health, relationships, and finance. This allows you to see which parts of your life require more attention and balance your efforts across different areas.

Use the Eisenhower Matrix

This is a powerful tool for prioritization. It divides tasks into four categories based on urgency and importance:

- Do First (urgent and important)
- Schedule (important but not urgent)
- Delegate (urgent but not important), and
- Don't Do (neither urgent nor important)

Apply this to your challenges and goals to determine what needs immediate action and what can be planned for later.

Set SMART goals

In the context of prioritization, ensure your goals are Relevant, and Time-bound so that you can see both what must be done to fulfil your purpose, and what must be done first.

Create a vision board

Make a vision board of images that visually represent your goals and aspirations. It serves as a daily reminder of what you're working towards and helps keep your focus aligned with your objectives.

Write a timeline

Draw a line across a sheet of paper and mark out specific deadlines. This not only provides a sense of urgency but also helps in tracking your progress and staying on schedule.

Use lists and planners

Break down larger goals into smaller, actionable steps and list them. Checking off completed tasks gives you a sense of accomplishment and momentum.

Leverage technology

Use apps and digital tools for task management, scheduling, and reminders.

Reflect and adjust regularly

Regular reflection on your progress is crucial. Assess what's working and what's not and be willing to adjust your strategies and goals as needed.

Seek feedback from mentors, colleagues, or peers

Sometimes, an external perspective can be invaluable. Don't hesitate to seek feedback to help categorize and refine your goals and strategies.

Embrace flexibility

While it's important to have a structured approach, it's equally crucial to remain flexible. Life can be unpredictable, and your ability to adapt to changing circumstances is a key component of success.

By employing these strategies, you can effectively prioritize and organize your challenges and goals. This makes them more manageable and approachable. This organization is not just about creating order; it's about empowering you to navigate your life's journey with clarity, purpose, and efficiency.

The seven-step framework to turn Goals into Achievements

Having worked out what Black Dots face you, what your purpose in life is, what goals you need to set to deal with your Black Dots and achieve your larger purpose, and what priority you should assign to your goals, now we are going to look at how you can turn those goals into achievements.

The seven-step process outlined here provides a comprehensive framework to turn goals into achievements. Each step plays a crucial role in the journey from planning to celebrating your progress. The steps are:

1. Plan
2. Prioritize
3. Take action
4. Monitor and adjust
5. Stay accountable
6. Adapt and evolve
7. Celebrate progress

Let's delve into each of these steps.

Step one: Plan

Begin by clearly defining your goals. What exactly do you want to achieve?

Based on these goals, develop strategies (the overarching methods) and tactics (specific actions) for achieving them.

Identify the resources you need and ensure they are accessible.

Step two: Prioritize

Determine the order of importance and urgency for your goals and the actions required to achieve them. Put high-impact actions first on the list.

Step three: Take action

Begin executing the tactics outlined in your plan. This is how you put strategies into practice.

Take action consistently and align your actions with the established plan.

Step four: Monitor and adjust

Regularly monitor your progress against your goals. Use trackable and measurable tactics for accurate assessment. Be prepared to adjust your strategies and tactics in response to feedback, challenges, or changes in circumstances.

Step five: Stay accountable

Hold yourself accountable for taking action and making progress. Self-discipline is key here.

Share your goals with others who can provide support and hold you accountable, like mentors, peers, or a support group.

Step six: Adapt and evolve

Stay open to changing your approach as you gain new insights, encounter different circumstances, or if certain tactics are not working as expected. Cultivate a growth mindset that views challenges and changes as opportunities for learning and improvement.

Step seven: Celebrate progress

You will have defined milestones along the path to achieving your goal, so be sure to acknowledge and celebrate your achievements, no matter how small. This helps you maintain your motivation and positivity.

Take time to reflect on what you have learned and how you have grown throughout the process.

Each of these steps represents a distinct and important phase in your journey towards achieving your goals. You start with a well-thought-out plan, prioritize what needs to be done effectively, take consistent action, monitoring and adjusting as needed, maintain accountability, be adaptable, and finally, celebrate each small step as you progress, so that you form a cycle that leads to successful achievement of your goals.

This structured yet flexible approach ensures that you not only reach your goals but also grow and evolve throughout the journey. However, your experience will tell you that life rarely moves in a straight, smooth line no matter how much thought we put into our analysis and our plans. So, let's turn next to how to deal with some of the obstacles that you are likely to encounter along the way.

Overcoming obstacles

Pursuing purpose-driven goals invariably involves facing challenges and obstacles.

I say that not to discourage you but to let you know that it is perfectly normal to stumble.

Obstacles test our resolve. Discipline and determination help us to overcome them.

These are the common obstacles you may face:

Procrastination

Often, we delay embarking on actions that will progress us towards our goals due to fear, uncertainty, or a lack of motivation.

Fear of failure

If you fear "failure"—which may well be a vague, undefined term for you—it can prevent you from taking the necessary steps towards your goals.

Lack of resources

Sometimes, the obstacle is external, such as a lack of time, money, or support.

Overwhelm

Feeling overwhelmed by the magnitude of a goal can lead to inaction or avoidance.

Changing circumstances

Life is unpredictable, and changing circumstances can disrupt even the best-laid plans.

The role of discipline in overcoming obstacles

Practicing discipline helps you to maintain consistent efforts towards your goals, even when your motivation is low, or the obstacles seem daunting.

A disciplined approach involves breaking down large goals into manageable tasks, making them less overwhelming and more achievable.

Discipline also involves adaptability—being able to adjust your strategies to deal with new challenges or changing circumstances.

Determination and resilience

Challenge your own preconceptions about what "failure" really means. It's about understanding that failure is a normal part of the process of tackling challenges and obstacles, and it offers a valuable learning experience. Then use determination to face your fear of failure, head-on.

When faced with obstacles, a determined mindset pushes you to find solutions and persist despite difficulties.

Determination is closely linked to resilience, the ability to bounce back from setbacks and to continue moving forward.

Practical Strategies for overcoming obstacles

Small steps

Focus on taking small, incremental steps towards your goals. This can help in overcoming procrastination and feeling overwhelmed.

Shift your mindset

Reframe obstacles as opportunities for growth and learning. Adopting a positive mindset can significantly change your approach to challenges.

Seek support

Don't hesitate to seek support from mentors, peers, or professionals. Sometimes, an external perspective can provide valuable insights and solutions.

Reflect and learn

Use setbacks as a chance to reflect and learn. What can you do differently next time? What lessons have these obstacles taught you?

Adjust your plan

Be willing to adjust your goals and action plans in response to the challenges you face. Flexibility is key to long-term success.

Pursuing purpose-driven goals is challenging for everyone and so exercising discipline and determination are vital in navigating these challenges.

By consistently applying effort, adopting a structured and adaptable approach, facing your fears, and learning from your setbacks, you can overcome obstacles and progress towards your goals.

And now, as we have frequently referred to the value of tracking that progress, let's take a deeper look at it.

Tracking Progress

I have mentioned the need for monitoring and acknowledging the advance you make towards your goals in quite a few places in this book, already. Now I am going to bring together, all in one place, the *Why* and the *How* of Tracking.

Why you should track your progress

Visibility is the principal reason why you should track your progress. It's highly motivating. It's encouraging to see how far you've come, especially in long-term projects.

Tracking your progress also helps you identify areas where you might be facing difficulties, allowing you to adjust your approach or seek additional resources. Be prepared to adapt your goals based on the progress you're making.

Use tracking as a tool for your own continuous improvement. It's not just about ticking off tasks but about evolving and refining your lifelong approach to goal achievement.

How you can track

Keep a journal for daily reflections on your progress to provide valuable insights. Note what you accomplished, what challenges you faced, and how you felt about your day.

Use your journal to record lessons learned and to brainstorm potential adjustments to your strategy.

Utilize digital tools and apps for task management. These can help in setting reminders, organizing tasks, and tracking deadlines. There are numerous apps designed specifically for tracking progress on various goals, whether they're related to fitness, learning, or project completion.

Break your larger goals into smaller milestones. This makes tracking progress easier, and each milestone achievement can be a cause for celebration.

Set yourself regular reminders—whether weekly, monthly, or quarterly, depending on the nature of your goal—to check in on these milestones.

Celebrate achievements

It's important to celebrate your successes, no matter how small, because each act of celebration boosts your motivation. Use these moments of celebration to reflect on what these achievements mean in the context of your larger goals and purpose.

So, systematically monitor your journey towards your goals, celebrate your achievements, learn from setbacks, and make necessary adjustments. Tracking your progress is fundamental to staying motivated, focused, and aligned with your purpose. Ultimately, this will lead you to the successful achievement of your goals.

Sometimes, sharing your progress with a trusted friend, mentor, or accountability group can motivate you. Next, we are going to look a little harder at the power of accountability.

The Power of Accountability

Sharing goals with others, or having an accountability partner, can significantly boost your sense of commitment and enhance the likelihood of your achieving your goals.

Finding someone to share your goals with is a strategy that leverages social dynamics and support systems to enhance the likelihood of achieving your objectives.

Partly it's to do with social accountability. When you share your goals with others, it creates a sense of external expectation. You have put your aspirations "out there." Knowing that someone else is aware of your goals and may check in on your progress can increase your commitment to those goals. The social pressure of not wanting to let others down, or to be seen as not following through on your commitments, is powerful.

An accountability partner can provide constructive feedback that helps you refine your approach and strategies. They can offer an objective viewpoint, helping you see things you might miss when you're too close to a situation. They can help identify blind spots in your planning or areas where you might be inadvertently sabotaging your efforts. They may also offer emotional support, which is crucial in maintaining motivation and perseverance, during challenging times.

Sharing your goals makes them seem more real to you. You hear yourself declaring them, in your own voice and your own words, and that has a powerful effect of reinforcing your sense of responsibility towards them.

Having regular check-ins with an accountability partner forces you to be more introspective and honest about your progress. They can also help you to recognize and celebrate your milestones, which in turn helps you maintain a positive outlook and motivation. Encouragement from someone who understands your goals and challenges can be a significant boost, especially when progress seems slow.

When you face obstacles, an accountability partner can offer you advice or help brainstorm solutions, drawing on their own experiences and perspectives.

People who leveraged the power of accountability

Let's explore some stories of individuals who have achieved their purpose-driven goals through the power of accountability. These stories illustrate how having someone to share your journey with can significantly impact your ability to reach your objectives.

Angela Duckworth—Grit and perseverance

Angela Duckworth is a psychologist known for her research on grit and perseverance.

Accountability in action

Throughout her research and writing process, Duckworth worked closely with mentors and peers who provided feedback and encouragement. This collaborative environment and the accountability it fostered were crucial for her to meet her goal to carry out her groundbreaking work on grit.

Outcome

Her research and subsequent book, *Grit: The Power of Passion and Perseverance*, have had a significant impact on how we understand success and perseverance.

Eric Yuan—Zoom communications

Eric Yuan is the founder of Zoom, a leading video communications company.

Accountability in action

Yuan's journey in building Zoom involved close collaboration and regular check-ins with his team. This accountability ensured that the company stayed true to its goals of delivering happiness and connectivity.

Outcome

Yuan's accountable leadership played a key role in Zoom's success, particularly highlighted during the increased demand for reliable video communication solutions.

Sheryl Sandberg—Lean In and leadership

Sheryl Sandberg was the COO of Facebook, and then of Meta, and is the author of *Lean In: Women, Work, and the Will to Lead*.

Accountability in action

Sandberg credits part of her success to her mentors and peers who provided honest feedback and held her accountable to her goals, both at Facebook and with her "Lean In" initiative.

Outcome

Her leadership at Facebook and the global impact of her book and the Lean In movement showcase the power of combining personal drive with accountable relationships.

Kathryn Minshew—The Muse

Kathryn Minshew, co-founder of The Muse, a career development platform.

Accountability in action

Throughout the development of The Muse, Minshew relied on a network of mentors and advisors. Their regular feedback and the accountability structure they provided were instrumental in navigating the challenges of a startup.

Outcome

The Muse has become a go-to platform for career advice and job searching, helping millions of people achieve their career goals.

Brian Chesky—Airbnb

Brian Chesky, co-founder and CEO of Airbnb.

Accountability in action

Chesky often speaks about the importance of mentorship and accountability in his journey. His decisions and strategies were often shaped through regular discussions with mentors and his co-founders.

Outcome

Airbnb's growth into a global platform that disrupted the traditional hospitality industry highlights the impact of accountable decision-making and leadership.

These real-life stories demonstrate how accountability—whether through mentors, peers, co-founders, or a supportive network—can play a vital role in achieving purpose-driven goals. These individuals not only pursued their visions with dedication but also leveraged the power of accountability to guide, refine, and realize their ambitions.

Celebrating milestones

As we explore the strategies you can adopt to ensure you achieve your goals and tackle your Black Dots, I need to emphasize, again, the importance of recognizing and celebrating small victories along the journey towards achieving larger goals.

Celebrating these milestones plays a crucial role in maintaining motivation, acknowledging progress, and building momentum because you:

- Acknowledge your progress
- Maintain your motivation
- Build your confidence and self-efficacy
- Create moments of reflection
- Foster a supportive environment
- Build momentum for your future goals

Let's look at each of those benefits, in turn.

Acknowledging progress

It's important to recognize your effort. Celebrating small victories is a way of acknowledging the effort and dedication that you have put into reaching those milestones. It's a recognition that every step forward, no matter how small, is an achievement in itself.

Celebration, after identification and recognition, makes your progress visible and tangible, which can be particularly motivating in long-term projects where the end goal may seem distant.

Maintaining motivation

Celebrations act as positive reinforcement, encouraging continued effort towards the next milestone. This reinforcement is key to maintaining enthusiasm and drive. The journey towards significant goals can feel monotonous or overwhelming. Celebrations introduce moments of joy and gratification that refresh and re-energize.

Building confidence and self-efficacy

Each small victory builds a sense of achievement. This boosts your confidence and your sense of self-efficacy, the belief in one's ability to achieve goals.

Celebrating achievements, especially in challenging projects, can help overcome feelings of self-doubt and reinforce the belief in one's capabilities.

Creating moments of reflection

It is important to pause, to reflect on the journey. Ask yourself, *how far have I come? Am I on the right road? Arm I going too fast? Too slow?*

Celebrations provide an opportunity to pause and reflect on the journey so far. This reflection offers you a chance to uncover valuable insights and lessons for your future endeavors. It also allows you to reassess your goals and your strategies to achieve them so that you can make adjustments based on what you've discovered.

Fostering a supportive environment

Celebrating milestones often involves sharing your success with others—family, friends, or colleagues. This shared celebration can strengthen support networks and foster a sense of community.

And don't forget that with this increased visibility, your celebrations can also inspire and motivate others around you who may be pursuing their own goals.

Building momentum for future goals

Each small victory contributes to a cumulative effect, building momentum towards the larger goal. Celebrating these wins keeps this momentum alive and well-recognized. The confidence and positivity you gain from these celebrations can be a source of encouragement when facing new challenges or setting new goals.

Celebration reinforces successful behaviors

So, we've established that celebrating your progress is a vital component in maintaining your motivation to pursue your goals. Celebrating your progress reinforces the behavior that led to that success.

The act of celebrating can trigger the release of the hormone and neurotransmitter, dopamine. It gives you an intense feeling of pleasure as part of the brain's reward system. The release of dopamine creates a positive emotional association with your achievement that, in turn, encourages you to continue your efforts.

Don't make the mistake of delaying the gratification you feel from celebrating. This is one area where it is not helpful to practice discipline and delay gratification in favor of achieving a longer-term goal. The act of celebrating smaller milestones along the journey towards a larger goal keeps the goal from feeling overwhelming and helps you maintain a sense of progress.

Celebrations can rejuvenate your energy and enthusiasm. They provide a much-needed break and a chance to recharge before tackling the next phase of your goal. Each time you celebrate a milestone, it builds your confidence in your ability to achieve. This growing confidence fuels further action and ambition.

Regular celebrations help cultivate a mindset of success. They shift the focus from "What have I still got to do?" to "What have I already accomplished?" This fosters a more positive outlook.

Celebrations also provide an opportunity to reflect on what worked well and what can be improved. This reflective practice is essential for learning and growth. By taking stock of your progress, you can make informed adjustments to your strategies, which is crucial for maintaining momentum and effectiveness.

Celebrating progress with friends, family, or colleagues can lead to increased support and encouragement from your social circle. And as other people see your progress, and how much you value it, your celebrations may inspire and motivate them. You encourage others in their pursuits.

Each celebration of your progress sets the stage for the next goal or milestone. It builds a foundation of success on which you can pursue future goals.

And talking of the future, regularly celebrating your progress keeps your long-term vision alive and vivid. That reminds you of the larger purpose behind your immediate goals.

Celebrating progress is more than just acknowledging your large and your small achievements; it's a critical strategy for boosting your motivation, sustaining your momentum, encouraging you to reflect and learn, foster social support, and set the stage for your future success. We're ensuring that the journey towards your goals remains dynamic, motivating, and fulfilling.

Think about your own Black Dot journey

So far, we've covered the concept of Discipline as a cornerstone of achievement. We've considered the importance of daily routines and habits, and how to use Accountability as a driving force to reach our goals.

To help you embed the Philosophy into your own outlook, I suggest you do this:

- Identify one daily routine or habit you'd like to establish or improve
- Describe the benefits of this routine and its alignment with your Black Dot challenge
- Create a plan to implement and track this routine
- Set clear accountability measures to ensure you stay on track
- Share your chosen routine, its benefits, and your plan for implementation
- Consider if holding yourself accountable has influenced your progress.

COMMIT TO YOUR ASPIRATIONS

Needless to say, I was beyond excited when I got the call offering me the opportunity to be the Managing Partner of the Central Coast General Office.

In my mind, this was the first step in my journey to ultimately reach my big, hairy, audacious Black Dot goal of earning $1,000,000 or more by age 50.

However, the reality of my new opportunity wasn't what I was expecting. After I accepted the promotion offer, they sent me a huge binder that had all the historical and current data of the General Office. I have to say that I was shocked when I went through the binder, especially the results from the previous year. As a Partner, I never took the time to look at company reports that were used to grade each of the 120 General Offices throughout the country. I was focused on one thing and one thing only: where I ranked on the promotability index that was used to determine future promotions.

The most surprising report I reviewed was called the General Office GPA rankings. The GPA report was created by the company using a formula that was developed with a "Grade Point Average" in mind.

There were several categories that were used to calculate the GPA of a General Office, similar to how we were all measured during our scholastic careers. However, I quickly learned GPA was an acronym for Growth, Profitability, and Accountability!

Just a subtle reminder that this was a business and not your college career. The Managing Partners were expected to "grow" the number of producers in the organization by hiring high-quality candidates and then retaining as many of them as possible, which would then improve the bottom line or "profitability" of the General Office. Last but not least was the "accountability" measurement. The Managing Partner of each office was responsible and accountable for increasing the General Office GPA annually.

After reviewing the Central Coast General Office GPA, I quickly realized that I had a huge Black Dot! Not only was the GPA one of the lowest in the entire company, but there also wasn't one category where the office was performing at a respectable level.

I observed several Black Dots when looking at the GPA report, but I decided that it was best to make the General Office GPA the Black Dot and then treat each category, like recruiting, retention, production, etc., as strategies as opposed to giving each of those categories their own Black Dot. Each of these several strategies had numerous tactics that would need to be implemented. By using the Black Dot Philosophy this way, it allowed me to assign one of my managers to each strategy and a group of agents and advisors in order to assist them with their individual objectives.

The next step would be the most important. When a new Managing Partner was promoted to a General Office, a VP from the Regional Office would introduce him or her to the entire General Office at an all-day meeting that generally consisted of several guest speakers who would give the agents and advisors product updates and sales ideas. That said, the primary reason for this all-day meeting was to introduce the team to their new leader and then the new Managing Partner would address all members of the General Office and outline a vision that hopefully everyone would support.

Prior to this big event, I was surprised to learn that the previous Managing Partner had never shared the General Office GPA with the team members. So I took the opportunity to explain to everyone how the General Office was measured, hoping that this would create a sense of pride and buy-in by each team member.

Fortunately, the response was extremely positive even after I told them that in the previous year we ranked near the bottom of the GPA rankings nationally. They were actually angry that this wasn't shared with them before, which is why they said the General Office lacked an "all for one and one for all" type of cohesiveness and spirit.

I then demonstrated how each one of them could have a positive impact on our "team" GPA and the future success of the General Office. I could feel their sense of pride and their desire to be part of a team! They vocalized not only their appreciation that I took the time to explain it to them, but many stood up to tell me they would do everything they could as individuals to have a positive impact on improving our GPA score by the end of the year.

I was astounded! Individually, they made public declarations which I believe is one of the most empowering things an individual and a team can do in order to create the mindset needed to live into their declarations.

Then it was my turn to do the same, but it was also my job to show them how. So I went through each category of the GPA methodically and had one of the expert guests close out each of those sessions with new sales ideas to equip each one of them with the tools they would need to improve their overall productivity over the previous year.

I closed my presentation by taking a huge risk. I had decided prior to this event that I would introduce them to The Black Dot

Philosophy. Previously, as a Partner, I had only shared it with my team, which was composed of about 15 agents and advisors. Now I was going to share it with over 100 members of the team with the hope they would embrace it.

I shared the story of how the Black Dot Philosophy was created and then took them through some examples of how they could use it to advance their careers. I explained to them that I used the Black Dot Philosophy for all of my personal and professional challenges and goals. I then gave them examples of how they could use it to not only improve their productivity but enhance their personal lives as well. I went on to explain that it would become the primary tool for both new and experienced agents and advisors and that it would become a huge part of our culture over time.

So over the next few months left on the calendar and then over the following calendar year, I made sure everyone was getting a report showing the General Office GPA and where we ranked nationally. We also used The Black Dot Philosophy as our primary coaching tool, and in turn, the agents and advisors used it to work through their own challenges and professional goals. That said, it was the inspiring stories that they shared with me about how the Black Dot Philosophy helped them in their personal lives.

Since I am a huge fan of declarations, both private and public, I declared at the start of the year that we would finish the year in the Top 10 of the GPA rankings. I shared with them the strategies and tactics we would implement as an office and in turn, I shared strategies and tactics I suggested that they should consider using in their professional practices. I then confirmed the challenge and updated them at each monthly team meeting. As we approached the 4th quarter, we were already in the Top 10 and were also in serious contention for several national trophies. Since we were in the 4th quarter of the year, I used a team sport, football, as an analogy. I shared stories and watched videos of some of the greatest victories by teams who won the game in the 4th quarter with only minutes and sometimes seconds in the game!

We also decorated the office with posters showing where we ranked with regard to the GPA and Trophy standings and updated them weekly. EVERYONE was on the same page and EVERYONE was working around the clock to contribute to the "team" effort to finish the year strong and win some national trophies.

The results were astounding! We finished that year with the most production in the history of the General Office, we finished the year with an almost perfect GPA, and we won five national trophies, including the President's Trophy for being the General Office with the highest increase in total production over a previous two-year average.

I will never forget the great agents, advisors, and managers of the Central Coast General Office. We made history together and had a lot of fun doing it. So don't be afraid to make big, hairy, and audacious goals (Black Dots), don't fear making public declarations and promises, and then celebrate your success. What really matters is challenging yourself and giving it everything you have, regardless of how you finish.

The Art of Declarations

We have already come across the fact that the simple act of declaring a commitment to our goals is a pivotal step in the journey towards achieving them. This declaration acts as a catalyst both as to the way you, yourself, think about your goals, and for the way others react and interact with them. The beneficial consequences of declaration are essential for successfully realizing your ambitions.

Now we are going to go deeper into this and find out why such declarations are so important in achieving your goals and why they are even more powerful when you make a commitment both publicly and to yourself.

Personal declaration

Start by declaring your commitment to yourself. This is a powerful affirmation and a promise you are making to the one person who matters: yourself. It clarifies and solidifies your intentions in your mind, making them more concrete and actionable, and strengthens your resolve. It is a powerful act of self-commitment. It reinforces your dedication to the goals you've set.

This private affirmation allows you to reflect on the alignment of your goals with your values and purpose. Use this opportunity for personal reflection. Understand deeply why these goals matter to you. Ensure that your pursuits are truly meaningful to you. This personal declaration is an integral part of building a committed mindset.

Public commitment

When you publicly declare your goals, whether to friends, family, colleagues, or a wider community, it increases your sense of accountability. Knowing that others are aware of your commitments can motivate you to follow through, as it adds a layer of external expectation.

Public declarations often open up avenues for social support and encouragement. These can prove vital during challenging times. Sharing your goals publicly can connect you with resources, advice, and opportunities that might not have been available otherwise. You might find others with similar goals, creating a community of mutual support.

Your declaration might also inspire others to pursue their own goals. You could be the catalyst for someone else's journey towards their ambitions.

The power of doing both

I strongly encourage you to declare your commitments both publicly and personally. Combining public and personal declarations offers a balanced approach. While public declarations provide external motivation and support, personal declarations ensure that your goals are deeply connected to your personal aspirations and values. Both forms of declaration reinforce your commitment from different angles, making it more likely that you will stay on track and overcome obstacles.

Enhancing your commitment

Each time you declare your commitment by speaking your goals out loud, you are making a commitment to yourself. It's a way of affirming your dedication to the pursuit and reinforcing your internal resolve.

Articulating your goals makes them more real and concrete, rather than leaving them as just ideas or wishes. It reinforces your intention to yourself and others and serves as a regular reminder of what you are working towards.

Regularly reaffirming your goals, both publicly and privately, can keep them fresh in your mind and maintain motivation. They remind you of your *why* and keep you aligned with your goals and serve as consistent reminders of what you're working towards, helping to maintain focus and momentum.

Creating a sense of urgency

Often, public declarations include timelines or deadlines. Setting these deadlines creates a sense of urgency and helps in prioritizing actions related to your goals. The urgency stemming from a public commitment can accelerate your actions and progress, keeping the momentum going.

Enhancing clarity and focus

Declaring your goals requires you to define them clearly and precisely. This process of articulation can help in refining your goals and making them more actionable.

With clear, declared goals, your efforts can be more focused and directed. It prevents you from straying off course and keeps you aligned with your objectives.

Building confidence

As you make progress towards these publicly and personally declared goals, your confidence and belief in your ability to achieve future goals will grow.

Publicly declaring goals can be an act of overcoming fear—fear of failure, judgment, or accountability. Facing these fears can build confidence and personal strength. There is an empowering aspect to declaring your goals. It's a statement of your ability and determination to achieve what you set out to do.

Creating a record of your journey

Your public declarations can become a record of your journey. Looking back on these can be incredibly rewarding, showing you how far you've come.

Coping with challenges

During times of doubt or challenge, revisiting your public and personal declarations can provide encouragement and remind you of the reasons behind your goals.

Networking and opportunities

Remember that you are connecting with like-minded individuals. By declaring your goals, you might connect with others who have similar objectives or who can offer assistance or collaboration opportunities. And sometimes, making your goals known more widely can lead to unexpected opportunities—advice from a mentor, perhaps, or partnership offers, or other resources.

Remember, the act of declaring your commitments is not just about making a statement. It's about setting yourself up for success. It's a commitment to yourself and an invitation for others to join in your journey. Whether your goals are personal, professional, health-related, or about contributing to a larger cause, declaring them can be the first step in a transformative journey.

So, I encourage you to embrace this step with courage and optimism—your declarations are the seeds from which your future successes will grow.

You see how much more likely it is that you will achieve your goals when you declare them, to yourself, and to other people. But it wouldn't be surprising if you feel a great deal of resistance to making a public declaration of your goals. The next thing we need to do is to address those fears.

Face the fear of making a public Declaration

First of all, we are going to acknowledge the range of fears that might prevent you from making a public declaration. Then we are going to consider some strategies to address them.

Fear of failure

Many people fear that declaring their goals may lead to public—and humiliating—failure. This fear often stems from a worry about not meeting expectations or being judged by others.

To combat this, it's important to reframe how you view failure. Instead of seeing it as a negative outcome, view it as a valuable learning experience and a natural part of the journey towards success.

Fear of being judged

The fear of being judged by others when declaring goals can be paralyzing. This often comes from a place of vulnerability and concern about the opinions of other people.

To neutralize this fear, focus on the support and positive feedback you can receive rather than potential negative judgments. Remember that most people are too focused on their own goals and challenges to judge yours harshly.

Fear of commitment

Declaring a goal can feel like making an overwhelming commitment, especially if the goal is significant or life-changing.

Manage the fear by breaking down your goal into smaller, more manageable tasks. This makes the commitment seem less daunting and more achievable and should make you feel braver about declaring it.

Fear of the unknown

The fear of stepping into unknown territory or changing one's life path can be intimidating when making a declaration.

Educate yourself as much as possible about the path ahead. Knowledge can reduce the fear of the unknown and empower you to take informed steps.

More strategies for overcoming fear

Start by making private declarations to yourself. This can build confidence and prepare you for more public declarations.

Initially, share your goals with a trusted circle of friends or family who are likely to be supportive.

Regularly visualize the successful achievement of your goals. Visualization can boost confidence and reduce anxiety.

Use positive affirmations to reinforce your ability to achieve your goals and overcome challenges.

Accept that the journey towards your goal may not be perfectly smooth. There will be ups and downs, and that's completely normal. Tackling your fear of making public commitments is one such "bump in the road."

Be prepared to adjust your goals and strategies as you progress; we have already seen the value of tracking your progress, so you know you have the power of adjustment based on data and evidence. If you adopt a flexible approach, you can reduce the pressure on yourself of the commitment you are making, and that will alleviate your sense of fear associated with declaring your goals publicly.

To sum up, overcoming any fears you may have of making public declarations involves acknowledging and addressing your fears. It may help you to know that it's extremely common to feel these fears. The way to tackle them is to find a strategy that helps you, such as reframing your concept of failure, starting by honing your declarations in private, building a support system, and practicing visualization and flexibility. You will find you can gradually overcome your fears and confidently make declarations that propel you towards your goals.

Embrace the Declaration Process

If you want to achieve your goals, you will find that it's vital to embrace the process of making personal and public declarations. Articulating your goals and stating your intention to reach them gives you clarity. You can't achieve what is not clear. But this is not an easy process so you may want to try out these strategies to help you embrace the declaration process.

Start with personal declarations
Begin by declaring your goals to yourself. Write them down in a journal, or speak them aloud during a personal reflection time. This step helps solidify the goals in your own mind before sharing them with others.

Create a supportive environment
Share your goals with people who support and encourage you. This might be close friends, family members, or a mentor. Their support can build your confidence in the declaration process.

Use positive affirmations
Develop affirmations that reinforce your commitment and ability to achieve your goals. Repeat these affirmations regularly to build self-confidence and reduce anxiety about declaring your goals.

Visualize successful outcomes
Practice visualization techniques. Imagine yourself achieving your goals and the positive outcomes that will result. Visualization can be a powerful tool in overcoming fear and embracing the declaration process.

Break down your goals
If declaring a large goal feels overwhelming, break it down into smaller, more manageable goals. Declaring these smaller goals can feel less daunting and more achievable.

Practice with a trusted individual
If you're nervous about making a public declaration, practice by sharing your goals with a trusted individual first. This can help you refine how you articulate your goals and build confidence for larger declarations.

Plan your declarations

Think about how you want to declare your goals. This might be in a formal setting: a meeting, for example, or a more casual conversation. Planning the setting and the way you'll make your declaration can ease anxiety.

Celebrate the act of declaring

Recognize and celebrate the act of making a declaration. Acknowledging this step as an achievement can reinforce its importance and make the process more rewarding.

Embrace flexibility

Understand that goals and circumstances can change. Embracing flexibility in your declarations can reduce the pressure and make the process more adaptable to your life's dynamics.

Reflect on past successes

Reflect on times in the past when you've achieved goals, especially those you've declared. This reflection can remind you of your capabilities and successes, bolstering your confidence in the declaration process.

Seek feedback and encouragement

After making declarations, seek feedback and encouragement. Constructive feedback can help you refine your approach, while encouragement can boost your morale.

This is how you can embrace the declaration process more confidently and effectively. I want to make it clear; this process is not just about announcing goals: it's about you setting the stage for your commitment, your accountability, and, ultimately, your achievement.

Declaring commitments has a profound influence on your mindset and in the next section, I want to explore the Ripple Effect that declarations have on your goals and your life.

The Ripple Effect of Declarations

Declaring your commitment is more than just telling people what goals you have set for yourself. The actual act of declaration affects the way you think about your goals. It sets up a ripple effect that extends beyond the initial act of declaration and shapes your approach to your goals and your life in general.

Let's explore the ripple effect in more depth so that you will see how valuable it is to embrace the act of making declarations.

Shift your mindset

Declaring your commitment shifts your mindset from mere intention to action. The act of declaration signals to yourself and others that you are serious about your goals, moving them from the realm of thought into the realm of action.

Once you declare your commitment, you will feel a heightened sense of responsibility and an obligation to follow through. This, in turn, fosters a more proactive and engaged mindset.

Change your behavior

Declaring your goals publicly can lead you to change your behavior to maintain consistency with your commitment. This is partly driven by a desire to align your actions with your words and partly because you are anticipating accountability.

Over time, the consistent actions taken to honor your declared commitments can lead to the formation of new, productive habits.

Enhance your focus and priority

Making a public declaration often requires you to clarify your priorities and focus. This clarity can then guide your daily actions and decisions, ensuring they align with your declared goals.

Knowing that you've made a commitment can reduce tendencies to procrastinate, as the declaration adds a layer of urgency to your goals.

Influence others

Your declaration can also influence those around you. It can inspire others to consider their own goals and commitments, creating a positive ripple effect in your social or professional circle.

Declarations often attract support from others who share similar interests or who are supportive of your goals, thereby building a network that can aid in your journey.

Reduce cognitive dissonance

The psychological principle of cognitive dissonance, the discomfort caused by holding conflicting beliefs or behaviors, plays a role here. Once you declare a commitment, you will experience a drive to reduce dissonance by aligning your actions with the commitment you've declared.

Build your confidence

When you successfully act on commitments you've declared, you will build confidence in your ability to set, and achieve, goals. This confidence, in turn, enhances self-efficacy—your belief in your ability to exert control over your own motivation, behavior, and social environment.

The benefits of the ripple effect of declaration are substantial. Declaring a commitment can transform your mindset, influence your behavior, clarify your focus, attract support, and enhance your self-efficacy. See how this transformation extends way beyond simply announcing your goals to influencing the broader aspects of your life and potentially the lives of those around you.

I'd like to dig a bit deeper into how your public declaration of your goals can inspire the people who surround you.

People who have made impactful declarations

These examples drawn from real life demonstrate the power of a well-articulated declaration in setting the stage for success.

Malathi Krishnamurthy Holla—Commitment to sports despite physical challenges

Declaration
Despite undergoing multiple surgeries and facing physical challenges due to polio, Malathi declared her commitment to excel in sports, particularly in para-athletics.

Impact
Her declaration led to a remarkable career in sports, earning her over 300 medals, including accolades in the Paralympics.

Chris Gardner—From homelessness to financial success

Declaration
Despite facing homelessness and financial hardship, Gardner declared his commitment to becoming a successful stockbroker and providing a stable life for his son.

Impact
His unwavering commitment and perseverance led him to become a successful entrepreneur and motivational speaker.

Maya Angelou—Commitment to writing and activism

Declaration
Maya Angelou, after overcoming a challenging childhood and years of silence, declared her commitment to expressing her experiences and advocating for civil rights through her writing and activism.

Impact
Her commitment led to a prolific career as a poet, author, and activist, inspiring millions and leaving a lasting impact on literature and social justice.

Jane Goodall—Environmental activism

Declaration
Jane Goodall declared her commitment to studying and protecting chimpanzees, beginning with her groundbreaking research in Tanzania.

Impact
Her declaration and actions revolutionized our understanding of primates, leading to significant advancements in conservation efforts and inspiring a global movement for environmental protection.

Jeff Bezos—Revolutionizing E-commerce

Declaration
Jeff Bezos declared his commitment to creating an online bookstore that would eventually become Amazon, revolutionizing the retail industry.

Impact
This declaration transformed the way we shop, leading to the development of one of the world's largest and most influential companies, significantly impacting global commerce and technology.

Each of these individuals made a powerful declaration of commitment that set the course for their remarkable achievements. These declarations were not mere statements of intent but were backed by consistent action and unwavering dedication, demonstrating the transformative power of a clear and passionate commitment.

How personal declarations can inspire those around us

These examples of common situations show how making personal declarations can inspire those around us.

Fitness and Health Goals

Example declaration

"I commit to running the marathon next spring by following a tailored physical training program and to eating a balanced diet."

The dedication of this person to training, their visible changes in health and fitness, and eventual participation in the marathon can inspire friends, family, and colleagues to pursue their own health and fitness goals.

Ripple Effect

This declaration can lead to a community running group, increased health awareness in their social circle, or even fundraising for a cause associated with the marathon.

Career and education aspirations

Example declaration

"I commit to advancing my career by acquiring a new certification in my field and seeking leadership opportunities within my organization."

A professional who declares their intention to pursue further education, such as a master's degree, or a new professional skill, and to go out of their way to find new responsibilities can motivate colleagues to consider their own career development.

Ripple Effect
This declaration can encourage a culture of continuous learning and responsibility-seeking within their professional network, leading others to explore educational opportunities or career advancements.

Personal development goals

Example declaration
"I commit to reading one book a month to expand my knowledge and understanding of different cultures."

An individual who publicly commits to a personal challenge, such as reading more widely about the world, and shares their progress, can inspire others to undertake their own personal development projects. This type of declaration fosters personal growth, intellectual expansion, and empathy.

Ripple Effect
Their journey can motivate others to explore and commit to their own passions or hobbies, leading to a wider culture of personal growth and exploration.

Environmental and social causes

Example declaration
"I commit to reducing my carbon footprint by using public transport, recycling, and supporting sustainable products."

When someone declares their commitment to an environmental or social cause—like reducing their carbon footprint or volunteering regularly—and shares their experiences and achievements, it can raise awareness and inspire others to take action.

Ripple Effect

This can lead to community initiatives, increased environmental consciousness, or greater involvement in social causes within their network. This kind of declaration can even contribute to broader environmental sustainability.

Overcoming adversity

Example declaration

An individual sharing their journey of overcoming a personal adversity, such as recovering from an illness or dealing with a difficult life situation, can be profoundly inspiring. Their declaration of facing these challenges head-on can provide hope and encouragement to others facing similar situations.

Ripple Effect

This can foster a support network, encourage open dialogue about difficult topics, and create a sense of community resilience.

In each of these examples, the act of declaring a personal commitment does more than just set the individual on a path toward their goal; it acts as a beacon for others. It demonstrates the power of commitment, the possibility of change, and the impact of taking action, thereby inspiring others to consider their own goals and what they might achieve through dedication and declaration.

We have taken a good, long look at the importance of declaring our commitments. I want to show you how to, first, craft a commitment and then, how to create a declaration. The two stages, commitment and declaration, are different and I will show you why, and why it is important to understand the difference.

The Anatomy of a strong commitment

We are going to take a look at how to craft clear and specific commitment statements.

A well-defined commitment statement is crucial for success in achieving your goal as it lays the groundwork for focused action and purposeful direction. You are aiming for crystal clarity. A clear commitment statement leaves no room for ambiguity. It precisely defines what you intend to do, eliminating confusion and helping you stay focused on the specific goal.

Clear commitments serve as a guide for daily decision-making. When your commitment is defined, you can easily assess whether your actions align with your goal. When you are faced with a choice of actions, you can discard those that don't help you to move further towards your goal.

When you make a specific commitment, you should include measurable objectives. For example, instead of saying, "I want to save money," a specific commitment would be, "I will save $200 every month." Now you are clear about how much money you want to save, and you have a time-frame in which to do it.

So, if you are standing in line for coffee and wondering if you should add that tempting piece of fragrant bear claw to your order, you might think, "I only have to save another $5 to get me to my savings target by next Friday. I'll pass on the pastry."

Talking of bear claw pastries reminds me to say it is a mistake to express your commitment as, "I will get healthier." The statement is too vague to action. What does "healthier" mean? How much healthier do you want to be. Reframe the commitment in clear and specific terms like this, "I commit to running three times a week for 30 minutes and to eating at least two servings of vegetables daily."

Being specific in your commitment translates your broader goals into actionable steps. This makes it easier to plan and do what you need to achieve your goals.

When your commitments are clear and specific, it's easier to track progress. This tracking can significantly boost motivation as you see tangible evidence of your advancement towards your goal.

Specific commitments increase your accountability to yourself and, if shared, to others. They provide a clear standard against which you and others can measure your progress.

Clear and specific commitments allow you to plan more strategically. They enable you to identify what resources, skills, and actions are necessary to achieve the goal.

As you progress towards your commitment, the specificity allows you to refine and adapt your strategies based on what is, or is not, working.

Specific commitments often lead to small wins along the way. When you celebrate those milestones, you are building your confidence and sense of achievement.

As you meet specific aspects of your commitment, it enhances your belief in your ability to meet commitments and achieve goals.

A clear and specific commitment should align with your broader life goals and values. This alignment ensures that the commitment is meaningful and contributes to your long-term vision.

When you have clear and specific commitment statements, they are more actionable, motivating, and effective in driving your progress towards achieving your goals. They serve as a foundation for focused effort, strategic planning, and personal growth.

Have you noticed how sometimes I talk of commitments, and sometimes of declarations? It is important to understand the distinction between them, as they are related, yet distinct, concepts in the journey towards achieving your goals. Let's find out what that distinction is.

The difference between a Commitment and a Declaration

A declaration is essentially an announcement or a statement of intent. It's about making your goals or plans known, either to others or to yourself. Declarations can be public (shared with others) or private (a personal acknowledgment). They serve as a way of stating, "This is what I plan to do or achieve. The act of declaring is often an initial step in goal-setting. It's about putting your intentions out there, setting the stage for action.

A commitment goes a step further than a declaration.

A commitment is a pledge or promise to take action toward the declared intention. It involves a deeper level of engagement and responsibility towards the goal. Commitment is more about an internal resolution and the determination to follow through on the declaration. It's a mindset of sticking to your plan, regardless of obstacles.

Commitment implies an ongoing process, a sustained effort towards achieving what you have declared. It represents the ongoing dedication and perseverance you are going to need to reach the goal.

Often, the process starts with a declaration. You state your goal. You might say, "I declare my intention to learn a new language." You follow your declaration with a commitment. "I commit to practicing this language for 30 minutes every day." Your commitment is your internal and ongoing resolve to achieve that goal.

Declarations can reinforce commitments. By declaring your intentions, you reinforce your commitment to those intentions.

While a declaration is about stating your intentions, a commitment is about your ongoing resolve and effort to realize those intentions. Declarations set the direction, while commitments are about the journey and the continuous effort to reach the destination set by the declaration. Both are crucial in the process of achieving goals, with declarations serving as the starting point and commitments ensuring the journey is seen through to completion.

We've spent some time learning how to frame our commitments. It's just as important to craft precise declarations if you want to set yourself up for effective goal pursuit. A well-crafted declaration not only articulates your intentions but also sets a clear direction for your efforts.

How to create precise Declarations

The first thing we need to do is to define your goal clearly. Be specific about what you want to achieve. There is overlap here with the way we talked about crafting specific commitments. Both commitments and declarations are headed towards helping you achieve your goal, so it makes sense that your goal, commitment, and declaration are going to be aligned.

So, instead of setting a vague goal like "I want to be healthier," specify what being healthier means for you, such as "I want to lower my cholesterol level to a healthy range" or "I want to run a 5K."

Include measurable elements in your declaration. For example, "I will run for one hour twice a week from now so that I can run the Trail Trotters 5k in September" is more precise than "I will run more."

Include a realistic but challenging timeline for your goal. A time-bound declaration creates a sense of urgency and helps in planning. For example, "I will complete my professional certification by the end of this year."

Instead of a general statement like "I will get fit," a precise, time-bound declaration would be "I commit to attending three fitness classes per week for the next six months to improve my overall physical health."

Ensure that your declaration aligns with your personal values and overall purpose. This alignment makes the goal more meaningful and motivating. For example, "I commit to volunteering ten hours a month, aligning with my value of community service."

Craft your declaration using positive and assertive language. Instead of saying, "I might try to learn a new language," say, "I will learn Spanish to a conversational level."

Consider making your declaration public, either by sharing it with friends, family, colleagues, or a broader audience. This can create a sense of accountability.

Whether or not you make it public, write down your declaration. Seeing it in writing makes it more real and tangible. You might put it somewhere visible as a daily reminder. Change around where you put it from time to time, to freshen up your attention.

Regularly review your declaration to remind yourself of your commitment. Reflect on its relevance and whether it still aligns with your changing circumstances or insights.

Create impactful and meaningful declarations

Now you know how to create precise goals and declare them, let's look at how you can craft impactful and meaningful declarations. This will help you take proactive steps that are aligned with your deep purpose and so towards your goals.

Reflect on your goals and values

Identify what matters. Begin by reflecting on what is truly important to you. What are your core values, passions, and long-term objectives? Understanding these will provide a foundation for your declaration.

Identify specific goals that align with these values and aspirations. Make sure these goals are meaningful and significant to you.

Define the scope of your declaration

Decide whether your declaration will address a long-term vision or a more immediate, short-term goal. Sometimes, starting with a short-term goal can build confidence and momentum.

Ensure that your goal is specific and clearly defined. Vague goals are less motivating and harder to commit to.

Craft a statement of commitment

Use clear, assertive language in your declaration. It should unequivocally state what you intend to do. Include measurable criteria and a time-frame; for example, "I commit to completing a 10K run in under 60 minutes by October this year."

Incorporate emotional significance

Your declaration should resonate on an emotional level with you. Why is this goal important to you? How does it connect to your personal values or life purpose?

Imagine you have achieved this goal. Hold that vision. How will you feel? Incorporate this emotional aspect into your declaration.

Write it down

If you haven't already, write your declaration down. This act of writing makes the commitment more concrete and tangible.

Keep your written declaration in a place where you can see it regularly. This constant reminder will reinforce your commitment.

Plan for action

Outline the initial steps you need to take to start working towards your goal. This makes the declaration actionable. Develop a broader strategy for how you will achieve your goal. Consider resources, potential challenges, and support systems. (Later in this book, we go into more detail on how to develop strategies and a plan to reach your goals.)

Share your declaration

Consider sharing your declaration with someone you trust, or even publicly. This creates a sense of accountability and can provide you with support and encouragement. When you choose your audience, though, be selective about who you share your declaration with. Ensure it's someone who will be supportive and who you feel comfortable being accountable to.

Review and adapt

Regularly review your declaration and the progress you're making. Is it still relevant? Are you on track? Be prepared to adapt your declaration if circumstances change or you gain new insights. The goal is progress, not rigidity.

How to declare your commitments

This is what you do when you are ready to declare your commitment, privately and publicly.

Declare your commitment privately

Start by declaring your commitment to yourself. You might say it out loud, write it in a journal, or find a personal ritual that signifies the importance of this commitment.

Prepare for a public declaration

Sharing your declaration with a supportive community helps you to solidify your sense of commitment and to build a support network.

Choose a platform or forum for your public declaration. This could be social media (Facebook, Instagram, LinkedIn, or X), a blog, a family gathering, or a meeting with friends or colleagues.

Plan what you will say or share. Craft text that outlines your commitment and why it's important to you. You might prepare a speech, write a post, or simply speak from the heart.

If you are writing a post, use hashtags related to your goals to connect with like-minded individuals or groups.

If you have a personal or professional mailing list, consider sharing your declaration in an email or your newsletter. This can be a more personal way to reach out to your network.

Make your public declaration

Share your commitment statement publicly. Be confident and clear about your goals and the steps you will take to achieve them. Express why these goals are important to you to give context and depth to your declaration.

Have a conversation with family and friends about your goals. Sharing with your close circle can provide a strong foundation of support. Consider hosting a small gathering or dinner to share your declarations in a more intimate setting.

Share your declaration in community groups, clubs, or gatherings you are a part of. This could be a fitness group, a book club, a professional organization, or a local community group.

If you enjoy writing, or making videos, consider starting a blog or a vlog to document your journey towards your goal. Share regular updates and insights. This method not only shares your declaration but also invites others to follow your journey, offering transparency and accountability.

If your goals are professionally oriented, consider sharing them with colleagues, mentors, or in professional networks. Sharing in professional settings can open up opportunities for support, mentorship, and collaboration.

Seek accountability and support

Ask for support from those you've shared your declaration with. This could be in the form of regular check-ins, encouragement, or sharing resources.

Consider finding an accountability partner or joining a support group related to your goal.

Join online forums or communities related to your goal. For example, if your goal is related to fitness, a fitness-focused forum, or a local sports club's social media group, could be ideal. These platforms often provide a supportive environment for sharing goals and receiving feedback and encouragement.

Share your progress

Regularly update your community on your progress. This not only maintains your accountability but also keeps your support network engaged and informed. Encourage feedback—this can provide valuable insights and different perspectives on your journey.

There are collaborative tools or apps designed for goal tracking and sharing, such as Trello, Asana, or habit-tracking apps. Some of these platforms allow you to share goals and progress with others so consider using them to maintain a sense of community support for your efforts.

The value of declarations

The act of declaring your goals is a powerful step in your journey towards achieving them. An impactful and meaningful declaration becomes a guiding force in your journey towards achieving your objectives aligned with your deep purpose. A precise declaration serves as a clear, motivating, and guiding beacon on this journey, and helps to focus your efforts and energies towards your intended outcome.

Much of what we have talked about so far is to do with what you think: We've seen how data, measurability, specificity, brings clarity to your journey to achieve your goals. But emotions—what you feel, what moves you at a deep and sometimes wordless level—play a significant role in fueling your motivation.

We are going to look into why you should deepen your emotional investment to sustain your efforts towards achieving your goals. Let's delve into how emotional investment in a commitment can deeply influence your drive and determination.

Deepen your emotional investment

The power of emotional investment

When commitment to a goal has personal significance for you, and resonates with your core values and beliefs, it evokes a stronger emotional response in you. This emotional connection makes the commitment more compelling and the pursuit more meaningful.

Emotions are a key driver of intrinsic motivation. When you are emotionally invested in a goal, the motivation to achieve it comes from within, making it more powerful and enduring.

Sustaining effort through emotional engagement

Emotional engagement with your goals helps sustain effort, even while you are battling obstacles. The emotional significance of the goal provides the resilience and grit needed to overcome challenges.

Strong emotional connections to your commitments foster a sense of resilience and determination. Emotions such as passion, pride, and a sense of fulfillment can help maintain your focus and drive.

Creating a vision tied to emotions

Imagine the successful achievement of your goals and the emotions associated with that success. How will you feel when you accomplish your goal? Happiness? Pride? Relief? This vision creates a powerful emotional pull towards the goal.

Acknowledge the emotional rewards that come with achieving your goals. Recognizing these rewards can serve as a significant motivator.

Harnessing positive emotions

Celebrate small victories along the way to harness positive emotions. This celebration not only acknowledges progress but also reinforces the positive feelings associated with success.

Cultivate feelings of gratitude and joy in your journey towards your goals. Positive emotions like these can fuel motivation and enhance overall well-being.

Dealing with negative emotions

It's natural to experience negative emotions such as frustration or disappointment during setbacks. Acknowledge these emotions, but also focus on learning from these experiences and moving forward.

Building emotional resilience is key to dealing with the ups and downs of pursuing significant goals. This involves maintaining a balanced perspective and staying committed despite emotional challenges.

Emotional connection as a guide

Regularly revisit and reassess your emotional connection to your goals. Are they still aligned with what you truly want and feel passionate about?

If your emotional connection to a goal changes, it may be a sign to adjust your commitment, or to redefine your goals, to better align with your current values and passions.

SUMMARY

The emotional connection to a commitment is a powerful motivator. It acts to sustain you in your journey towards achieving goals. This emotional aspect fuels your intrinsic motivation, sustains your effort through challenges, and provides a deeper sense of fulfillment and purpose in the pursuit of your goals. Embracing and understanding the emotional dimensions of commitment can lead to a more engaging, rewarding, and successful goal achievement process.

You will want to know how to enhance your motivation and commitment as you begin your journey to achieve your goals. Let's try some exercises to connect deeply with your goals on an emotional level.

Connect deeply with your goals on an emotional level

Visualize

Take a quiet moment to close your eyes and vividly imagine achieving your goal.

Picture the scene in detail—where are you, who is with you, what are you doing? How do you feel? Joy, pride, satisfaction, relief? Something else?

Focus on the emotions you feel in this visualization. Whatever it may be, let yourself experience these emotions fully.

Journal

Write about why your goal is important to you. What does achieving this goal mean on a personal level? How does it align with your values or life purpose?

Regularly journal about your emotional responses related to your progress. Note feelings of excitement, challenges, and how you overcome them.

Illustrate

Create a physical vision board that represents your goal. Include images, quotes, and symbols that resonate with your goal and its significance to you. Place the vision board where you'll see it daily as a visual reminder of your goal and the emotions connected to it.

Practice gratitude

Each day, identify and write down aspects of your goal pursuit for which you are grateful. This could be progress made, lessons learned, or the support you've received.

Appreciate the journey itself. This practice helps in recognizing and appreciating the journey towards your goal, not just the destination.

Write a letter

Write a letter to your future self, describing what you have achieved, how you got there, and how it makes you feel. Be as descriptive and emotional as possible. Set reminders to revisit this letter periodically and reread it to remind yourself of the emotional significance of your goal and to renew your motivation.

Meditate

Engage in a meditation where you focus your thoughts on your goal. Consider the deeper meaning behind your goal and the positive impact its achievement will bring.

Be aware of the emotions that arise during this meditation and embrace them. Acknowledge how these emotions drive your commitment to your goal. Remember to note what you've discovered in your journal.

Storytelling

Imagine you are narrating the story of your journey towards your goal. How would you describe the challenges, the triumphs, and the emotional highs and lows? If comfortable, share this story with a trusted friend or family member. Speaking about your journey can deepen your emotional connection to your goal.

Connecting with role models

Identify individuals who have achieved similar goals. Learn about their journeys, the challenges they faced, and how they felt upon achieving their goals. Reflect on how their stories resonate with your own aspirations and emotions.

If you engage in these exercises, you will deepen your emotional connection to your goals. This will enhance your motivation and give you the drive you need to achieve them. These practices help to keep you aware of your deepest emotions in response to your goals. Your awareness keeps your goals vibrant and emotionally resonant. That will make the journey towards achieving them more engaging and fulfilling.

Think about your own Black Dot journey

So far, we have looked at how declarations and promises can reshape your mindset. We have looked at some real-world examples of impactful declarations and considered declarations as a driving force behind success.

To help you embed the Philosophy into your own outlook, I suggest you do this:

1. Write down declarations related to your Black Dot challenge
2. Craft promises that reinforce your commitment
3. Reflect on how declarations can transform doubt into conviction
4. Share your experience with making declarations and how they have influenced your mindset.

STEP
4

CRAFT YOUR GAME PLAN

In the early days of my career, I made a Black Dot declaration to myself, and I kept this particular Black Dot private, even though I am a strong believer in making public declarations. I didn't feel I needed to share this one publicly. You will soon find out that making a declaration to yourself might be the only declaration you need to make.

As you know, I made a declaration and commitment to myself that I was going to earn a million dollars or more by the time I turned 50. This would be my biggest Black Dot challenge until 2014 when I faced a life or death situation that was totally unexpected. I will share that story with you later in the book.

As I have also shared with you, to earn a million dollars or more, you would need to be managing one of the larger General Offices in the company, and there were probably about 10 of them at that time where a million dollars or more of personal income was a possibility.

Four years after I was promoted to Managing Partner of the Central Coast General Office, I got another call about an opportunity to manage a larger General Office in San Jose, California. I always looked at these new opportunities as a way of giving back to the company.

When a General Office opened up, it was typically because that office was not performing at a level that was expected. It certainly wasn't the case 100% of the time, as there are a lot of other reasons that could cause an office to be available. That said, I was never offered an office that was performing really well, so that should give you some added perspective.

The General Office in San Jose was in serious trouble, and the company needed a strong Managing Partner to turn that ship around. I was always flattered to get that call, and I also felt an obligation to accept the challenge even though it wasn't a requirement.

As I shared with you earlier, if you wanted to continue to exponentially grow your income, you would typically need to manage a larger office with a lot of upside potential. The San Jose General Office definitely had the potential to grow into one of the largest offices in the company when you just consider where it was located. By the way, I would later change the name of the office to the Silicon Valley General Office since the city of San Jose was now being referred to as the "Silicon Valley".

I'm going to fast forward five years after I took over the Silicon Valley General Office. During that five-year period, we broke just about every General Office record, and we won multiple national trophies as well. Again, I was at the top of the Promotability Index, and so I wasn't surprised when I got the call. What I didn't know was that it would change my life in so many ways, both personally and professionally.

It was 2006, and life was good! My income had shot up to over $450,000, and I believed that I could continue to grow my income to meet my goal of $1,000,000 by age 50. I was going to be 48, and getting to the $1,000,000 goal in two years was certainly a possibility.

I bought a beautiful home, and I was in a relationship with a really wonderful woman. The last thing that was on my mind at that time was taking over another General Office and moving again. Another reason for staying put in California was a provision that I had negotiated in the custody agreement with my former wife several years earlier. It stipulated that when my son turned 14, which was only five months away, he could decide for himself where he wanted to live for the next few years, and he absolutely loved California.

In December of the previous year, I was driving with the top down on a perfect 70-degree day to the home office of one of my advisors who lived in the foothills on the way to Santa Cruz. The drive was one of the most beautiful in the entire State of California. Just as I was pulling up to the advisor's home, my cell phone lit up, and I could see the call was coming from our Corporate Headquarters in Manhattan.

It was the Vice Chairman of the Company, and he called to offer me another promotion to an even bigger office than Silicon Valley. However, I really wasn't feeling it for all the reasons I gave you, plus it turns out this new opportunity was located just outside of Cleveland, Ohio. I was born in Cleveland. I had watched the family movies of me and my sister playing in the snow! I quickly made up my mind and told the Vice Chairman that I was going to stay put in Silicon Valley.

What he said next really surprised me. I think he was anticipating that I might turn down the offer, so he did his homework. The company really needed me, as the two previous Managing Partners had been terminated within a few months of each other due to highly unusual circumstances. This had created a toxic environment, and they needed to get a new Managing Partner there quickly. They also needed someone with a track record of turning around offices that were in a similar state of toxicity. It wasn't all that long ago that this particular General Office was an elite General Office and was ranked in the Top 10, but it had recently fallen back and wasn't even in the Top 20. The company needed someone who could stop the bleeding and turn the office around. I was that guy, and they knew it!

After a long pause, he said, "Jerry, doesn't your son Tyler live near Toronto, Canada?" He then said, "Toronto is close enough to Cleveland that you could drive there and spend weekends with him and just think how much easier it will be for him to see you versus that long flight to California!" Admittedly, I was floored that he knew this, but I quickly responded with, "While everything you have said is true, my son will most likely decide when he turns 14 in a few months that he is going to move to California to live with me. Quite frankly, if I am living in Cleveland, he will probably choose to stay where he is until he graduates from High School."

I expected him to respond by saying he understood the issue, but he was one smart man! He then said, "Are you 100% sure that's what he is going to decide to do?"

The truth is that I didn't know, as it wasn't something I ever discussed with him or that he had to even think about until he turned 14, and that was still several months away. But I gave him a response he deserved. I said, "You make a good point. Let me reach out to my son, and I'll tell him the situation (Black Dot) and see if he is leaning one way or another." So we agreed I would get back to him in a few days with my final answer.

Now, I was very confident that if my son was going to choose to live with me, he would 100% want to live in California. So I called him and explained the situation to him. I asked him if taking the promotion and moving to the Cleveland area would impact his decision. By the way, I was very careful to let him know that I was not asking him to make a decision now, but I had a responsibility to him to share the decision I was being asked to make. I told him that if he was leaning toward living with me, I would stay put in California and turn down the promotion. If not, I would still turn down the offer as the General Office was doing really well and because he could continue to spend his non-school time enjoying our time together in sunny California. He loved the beach, loved to go snowboarding in Tahoe and Mammoth plus he had family and early childhood friends that he could spend time with as well.

He then confirmed what I already knew, that if he decided to move in with me, he wanted to live in California. He also said that he wasn't even close to making a decision. It was at that moment, I decided to turn down the offer so I could stay in California for all the reasons I have shared with you.

The next day, just as I was preparing to call the Vice Chairman to turn down the offer, my son called me. What he said to me on that call blew my mind! It went something like this, "Dad, I thought about your situation and I would like to make a proposal. I have not decided where I want to live when I turn 14, but I think you should take the promotion". He then said, "regardless of my decision, whether I stay in Canada or move in with you, if you are in Cleveland, you and my mom will be living much closer to each other. That means it will be much easier to see either one of you, and this way, it won't really matter where I'm living because it will only be a short plane ride to see both of you."

Needless to say, I was so proud of him for thinking it through like he did and how well he articulated a scenario that was a win-win for all involved!

After we got done talking, I called the Vice Chairman and accepted the offer! It would turn out to be the best decision I would ever make, thanks to my son.

My son ultimately decided to stay in Canada, and I totally understood why he made that decision. He now had two siblings that he adored, he had a ton of friends that he had known for many years, and I think he had a schoolboy crush on a girl who was in his marching band. All good reasons for a 14-year-old to stay put.

That said, at the end of the day, I am pretty sure the Black Dot played a big role in his decision making process. I shared the Black Dot with him as he was growing up, and instead of developing strategies and tactics that could be somewhat complicated to tackle his Black Dots, I shared the +/- problem-solving tool that has been around forever. It's one that I even use today when I'm conflicted about something. You simply put all the reasons why you should do something you're trying to decide under the + sign and all the reasons why it's not a good idea under the - sign. Then it's a matter of which side has the most reasons for doing or not doing whatever it is you are trying to solve. I never asked him, but my guess is that is how he came up with the solution to my dilemma! To say I was proud would be an understatement!

The career change was also a blessing. The Northern Ohio General Office was composed of some of the best human beings I've ever known, and their response to me was amazing. They were hungry for new leadership, and they also had a tremendous amount of pride in the great history of the General Office.

Together, we generated one of the quickest turnarounds in the history of the company. By the time I left six years later, the Northern Ohio General Office was once again one of the premier General Offices in the company.

You might be wondering what happened to my big, hairy, audacious Black Dot goal of earning $1,000,000?

My income the year I turned 50 was $1,150,000! In fact, my average annual earnings were in excess of $1,000,000 until my retirement from the company in 2018.

I also want to share that the move to Northern Ohio allowed me to see my son way more than if I had stayed in Silicon Valley. What's really quite funny is that when he turned 18, he decided to go to college in Santa Barbara, California, where he graduated from UCSB with a degree in communications. He is now 32, lives in San Diego and is incredibly successful. We are also about as close as a father and son can be, and I am so blessed to have a son like him.

Examples of notable figures who have successfully crafted and executed their game plans include:

1. **Indra Nooyi**: Former CEO of PepsiCo, known for her strategic thinking and leadership in transforming the company.
2. **Frederick W. Smith**: CEO of FedEx, who revolutionized the logistics industry with innovative strategies.
3. **Vera Wang**: Transitioned from a career in journalism to becoming a renowned fashion designer, showcasing the importance of adaptability and strategic planning.
4. **Richard Branson**: Founder of the Virgin Group, known for his innovative approaches and willingness to take risks.
5. **Serena Williams**: Her strategic planning and mental fortitude on and off the tennis court make her a prime example of crafting a game plan for success.

Use Strategy and Tactics to achieve your goals

We have spent a good amount of time on how to define your goals, and we've gone in depth into how you begin your journey to achieving them. Now we are going to look at strategies and tactics (and the difference between them) for making sure that with planning and execution, you do achieve them.

I'm going to show you how to utilize both strategies and tactics in the pursuit of your goals. Understanding and mastering the art of balancing these two elements is crucial for effective planning and execution.

The distinction between a Strategy and a Tactic

Think of Strategy as a framework for making decisions. It's the overarching plan that guides your actions and moves you closer to your goal. It's about the bigger picture of what you want to achieve, being aligned with your long-term vision, and is informed by your values, aspirations, and the bigger picture.

Tactics are the specific short-term actions, steps, or tasks that you undertake to fulfill the strategy. They are the practical, on-the-ground tasks that move you toward your goal. They home in on the detail of how you will achieve the broader aims outlined in your strategy. While strategies provide the overall direction, tactics need to be adaptable and responsive to the immediate situation and feedback.

Let me show you the difference between strategy and tactics in these examples.

If you run a business that has a goal to increase its market share, you might adopt a strategy to enhance its brand recognition. The tactics you employ to fulfill the strategy could include working on a targeted social media campaign, making partnerships with influencers, and putting on promotional events.

If, in the personal arena, you have a goal to improve your well-being, you might adopt a strategy to cultivate a balanced lifestyle. The tactics you employ to fulfill that strategy might involve scheduling regular exercise, practicing mindfulness, and ensuring a healthy diet.

Both strategies and tactics need to be grounded in reality. They should be realistic and achievable, taking into account your resources, constraints, and external environment. Tactics should be measurable and trackable, allowing for monitoring progress and making necessary adjustments.

A balanced approach is crucial, where you use short-term tactics as stepping stones towards your strategic vision.

The Interplay Between Strategy and Tactics

There's a dynamic relationship between strategy and tactics. Effective tactics contribute to the strategy, and a sound strategy guides the selection and implementation of tactics. For successful goal achievement, your tactics must align with and support your strategy. Each tactical action should be a step towards the strategic objectives.

Tactics provide feedback on the effectiveness of the strategy. This information can be used to adjust both tactics and strategy as needed. Use the feedback from tactical execution to refine and adjust your strategy. This feedback loop is essential for continuous improvement and responsiveness.

Measure and evaluate strategies and tactics

Regularly track the progress of your tactics and evaluate the effectiveness of your strategy. Are the tactics yielding the desired results? Is the strategy leading you towards your goal?

Be prepared to make adjustments. If certain tactics aren't working, modify them. If the strategy needs refinement, update it, based on your learnings.

It's important to understand how these two components, strategy and tactics, work together to achieve goals. It involves careful planning, execution, and the ability to adapt both strategies and tactics in response to progress and changing circumstances. Mastering this art is key to effectively turning your goals into reality.

There are different types of strategies: Long-term versus Short-term; Holistic versus Specific; Adaptive versus Prescriptive.

Let's look at each type, so you can be more effective in planning and executing actions that align with your goals.

Long-term strategies

Long-term strategies are vision-oriented. They are designed to achieve broader, more ambitious goals. They represent your overarching vision and are aligned with core values and long-term aspirations.

These strategies span a longer period, typically years. They require patience, persistence, and a sustained effort.

While they provide a clear direction, long-term strategies also require flexibility so you can adapt them to changing circumstances, new information, and evolving goals.

Long-term strategies often involve building foundations that will support future achievements, such as developing skills, creating networks, or establishing systems.

Short-term strategies

Short-term strategies focus on achieving more immediate objectives. They are typically more specific and narrowly focused than long-term strategies.

These strategies are designed for quicker implementation and results, often within a few weeks to a year.

Some short-term strategies are stepping stones towards long-term goals. Each one helps you get part, but not all, of the way. They often involve achieving more immediate tasks that contribute to the bigger picture.

Due to their shorter duration, they can be measured and adjusted more frequently. This allows for quick feedback and the ability to respond to immediate challenges or opportunities.

Interplay between long-term and short-term strategies

Where you employ a combination of long-term and short-term strategies, it's crucial that your short-term strategies align with and support the achievement of the long-term strategies. They should not be in conflict with each other. You must aim for them to complement each other.

It's easier for you to see the difference by looking at some examples. Suppose you are considering your career development. A long-term strategy might be to become a leader in your field. Short-term strategies could include taking specific courses, attending workshops, or completing a particular project that enhances your skills and knowledge relevant to your field.

Or suppose you want to improve your health. If your long-term strategy is to lead a healthier lifestyle, short-term strategies might involve starting a specific diet plan, joining a gym, or training for a 5K run.

A balanced approach involves having both long-term and short-term strategies working in tandem. The long-term strategies set the direction, while short-term strategies provide a framework for the immediate actions.

Successful short-term strategies can build momentum and provide motivation and resources that fuel long-term strategies.

Understanding and knowing how to balance long-term and short-term strategies are key to successful goal realization. Long-term strategies provide the vision and overarching direction, while short-term strategies give you a framework for dealing with the immediate, actionable steps. Together, they form a cohesive plan that guides you from where you are now to where you want to be in the future.

The difference between holistic and specific strategies

There are holistic strategies and there are specific strategies. Understanding the difference between them is crucial for an understanding of how to approach goal-setting and achievement. Each type of strategy plays a unique role in the overall planning and execution process.

Holistic strategies

Holistic strategies take a wide-ranging approach. They consider the big picture, for example, your whole life, and how different elements of a plan interact with and impact each other.

In a holistic strategy, the focus is on achieving balance and synergy. In personal development, this might involve balancing your career ambitions with your personal well-being, family time, and other life aspects.

These strategies often involve long-term vision and planning. They are about creating a cohesive and harmonious approach to achieving overarching life goals.

Holistic strategies require adaptability and an integrated approach, considering how changes in one area affect the whole.

Specific strategies

Specific strategies are more narrowly focused. They concentrate on achieving a particular goal or task that often has a well-defined scope and clear, measurable objectives.

These strategies are detailed, action-oriented, and often short-term. They outline specific steps and actions required to achieve a particular objective.

Specific strategies are designed to have a direct and immediate impact. For instance, in a business context, this might involve a strategy to increase sales in a particular quarter.

Interplay Between Holistic and Specific strategies

Holistic and specific strategies should complement each other. Holistic strategies set the overall direction and ensure balance, while specific strategies focus on achieving individual objectives that contribute to the broader vision.

Specific strategies can be seen as components or subsets of holistic strategies. They are the building blocks that, when combined, support the holistic strategy.

A holistic strategy might involve an overall goal of achieving a healthy lifestyle. Specific strategies within this could include a diet plan for weight loss, a workout regimen for fitness, and meditation practices for mental health.

In a business context, a holistic strategy could be overall business growth and market expansion. Specific strategies might include launching a new product line (product strategy), expanding into a new geographic market (market strategy), or enhancing digital marketing efforts (marketing strategy).

Holistic strategies are about the big picture and the interconnection of various life aspects, or business components. They focus on overall harmony and long-term vision. Specific strategies are more narrowly focused, detailing the steps to achieve particular objectives. Both are essential, and their effective integration is key to a well-rounded and successful approach to achieving goals and objectives.

Adaptive versus Prescriptive strategies

Adaptive strategies are flexible and evolve based on changing circumstances, feedback, and new information. They are designed to adjust as needed. Prescriptive strategies are more defined and structured. They outline specific actions and prescribe a clear plan based on an initial analysis or theory.

An adaptive strategy involves continuous monitoring and learning. It acknowledges that environments are dynamic and that strategies must be responsive to remain effective. Adaptive strategies often encourage innovation and creative problem-solving, as they need to be tailored to evolving situations. They are particularly useful in uncertain or rapidly changing environments where fixed plans may quickly become outdated.

Prescriptive strategies, being defined and structured, work well in stable and predictable environments where variables and outcomes are more controllable and foreseeable. Prescriptive strategies can be more efficient in the short term as they provide clear guidelines and a set course of action. They are often based on established best practices or proven methods and are ideal when a clear path to the goal is known.

Interplay between Adaptive and Prescriptive strategies

While prescriptive strategies can set the initial course, adaptive strategies allow for necessary adjustments and refinements based on real-world feedback.

You may start with a prescriptive strategy and, as you gather more information and encounter different situations, transition to a more adaptive approach. Let's use an example in personal goal-setting. You might start with a prescriptive strategy for a fitness plan so that you can get the journey towards your goal of personal fitness underway but adapt it as you learn more about your own pace, preferences, and challenges.

There are circumstances where you might want to start with an adaptive strategy before introducing a prescriptive strategy. For example, a startup might use an adaptive strategy because it wants to constantly learn from customer feedback and observe market trends so that it can refine its business model. Conversely, a well-established corporation might employ more prescriptive strategies for efficiency and consistency in its operations.

Adaptive strategies are characterized by their flexibility and responsiveness to change, making them suitable for uncertain and dynamic environments. Prescriptive strategies, on the other hand, are more structured and defined, working well in stable and predictable situations. Whether you choose an adaptive or a prescriptive strategy depends on the nature of the environment, your goals, and the degree of certainty or predictability associated with them.

Effective planning involves a blend of both, allowing for structure and adaptability as circumstances evolve.

To implement strategies, we need to use tactics. Let's dive into those now.

Understand Tactics so you can implement Strategies

Tactics are the specific, practical steps taken to implement strategies. They are the actionable components that bring your strategies to life. Unlike the broader approaches outlined in strategies, tactics are detailed and concrete, outlining exactly what will be done, by whom, and, often, by when.

Suppose you have a goal to increase your rate of hydration by drinking six glasses of sparkling water daily by a date three months from now. Your strategy might be to solve the issue that you forget to drink water because you are so busy. Your tactics are to buy a regular supply of water from a place that has emotional resonance for you; to replace two cups of coffee that you usually drink in the afternoon with water; and to buy six high quality drinking tumblers that make it a pleasure to drink something as mundane as water from.

You now know what will be done and who is doing it. If you add a deadline to get the water and the glasses in place by next Friday, then you also know by when. Your tactics are in place.

Measurable tactics have quantifiable results. They allow you to define success in specific, numerical terms. By Friday, you bought the water, and bought the glasses. By the end of two months, you're drinking four glasses of water each day. You're on track to getting six glasses down a day by the end of three months.

In creating measurable tactics, you are setting benchmarks. You had no water, now you have water.

To change the example, you might be looking at a sales strategy. A measurable tactic to employ might be "to increase monthly sales by 15%." The 15% provides a clear target to measure against.

Measurable tactics enable you to evaluate the effectiveness of your actions. You can clearly see whether the tactic is achieving the desired result by looking at when you started and when you finish, two points in time compared to each other.

Continuing with the idea of measurability, you'll also need to be able to monitor progress over time. Trackable tactics enable you to do this. They let you focus on the course of ongoing progress. They are about setting up systems or processes that allow you to track your actions and their outcomes.

When you apply trackable tactics, it's important to observe consistently. For instance, a trackable tactic in a marketing campaign might involve monitoring website traffic daily or weekly. This does not just measure the end result but tracks progress and patterns over time.

Trackable tactics are valuable for making adjustments. By consistently observing progress, you can make informed decisions about whether to continue, modify, or halt a tactic.

Let's look at a couple of examples. If your goal is to improve fitness, a measurable tactic might be "to run a total of ten miles per week." A trackable tactic could be "to record daily running distances and times to monitor progress and adjust training as needed."

Another example might be seen in this project to improve customer satisfaction. A measurable tactic was set up "to achieve a customer satisfaction score of 90%." The trackable tactic was "to monitor customer feedback weekly to identify areas for immediate improvement."

While adopting both measurable and trackable tactics is essential, note how they serve slightly different purposes. Measurable tactics help you assess if a specific outcome was achieved. Trackable tactics give you ongoing insight into how well a tactic is performing.

Employing both types of tactics in your plan allows for both end-point assessment (measurable) and ongoing adaptation (trackable). Both types are essential for effectively implementing your strategies. Measurable tactics provide clear targets for success, while trackable tactics offer insights into ongoing performance and the opportunity for timely adjustments.

In complex and dynamic environments where conditions and challenges can change rapidly, you need tactics that allow for a more nimble and effective approach. This is why we now need to meet two types of tactic, Adaptive and Responsive, that help you to achieve goals amid uncertainty.

Let me explain what they are, and the difference between them, so that you can respond with the right type of tactic for the situation.

Adaptive tactics

Adaptive tactics are those that can be modified or adjusted in response to changing circumstances, feedback, or new information. They are flexible and evolve as the situation demands.

These tactics involve anticipating potential shifts in the environment and being prepared to alter the approach accordingly.

In a business context, an adaptive tactic might involve regularly revising marketing strategies based on consumer trends. In personal fitness, it could mean adjusting your workout routine based on feedback from your body, such as when you suffer injury, or your fitness levels change.

Responsive tactics

Responsive tactics are those that are specifically designed to react to and address current situations or immediate challenges. They are more about responding effectively to the present conditions.

These tactics require real-time adjustments and quick decision-making to deal with current challenges or to take advantage of immediate opportunities. For example, in a customer service setting, a responsive tactic could be addressing customer complaints or feedback as they arise. In project management, it might involve swiftly addressing unforeseen issues during a project's execution phase.

Flexible and agile

Both types of tactics, adaptive and responsive, prioritize flexibility and agility. They necessitate a readiness to change course as required. They involve continuous monitoring of the environment, situation, or progress to identify when changes or responses are needed.

Adaptive tactics are more proactive, preparing for potential changes, while responsive tactics are more reactive, dealing with situations as they arise.

A strategic combination of both adaptive and responsive tactics can be highly effective. While adaptive tactics prepare you for potential future changes, responsive tactics equip you to deal with immediate issues.

Ensure that both adaptive and responsive tactics align with your overall strategy and long-term goals. They should not derail you from your primary objectives.

To sum up, adaptive and responsive tactics are about enabling you to adjust and react effectively to change and immediate challenges. Adaptive tactics prepare you for potential future shifts, while responsive tactics enable you to address current issues effectively. If you use a mix of both, in alignment with your overall strategy, you will find it easier to navigate dynamic environments and still achieve your goals.

We have looked at what strategy is, and at what tactics are, and at the different types of strategy and tactics that can help you to pursue your goals. Now we need to spend a little more time exploring the relationship between strategy and tactics and why it is important for them to aligned.

Align tactics with strategy

Every tactic you employ should be a step towards achieving your strategic goals.

Think of the tactics you employ as the actions you take on a day-to-day basis. Each of these actions must directly contribute to the larger, overarching plan or you will waste your energy in haphazard pursuit of your goals.

The tactics should not only support but also be consistent with the strategy. There should be a clear and logical connection between what you do (your tactics) and the framework you have put in place to reach your ultimate goals (strategy).

Think of your strategy as the guiding framework, or the *what* and the *why* of your goals. It provides the direction and the reasons behind your pursuit. Taking our cue from an earlier example, the strategy to rehydrate might be "I need to drink more water (*what*) because my state of dehydration is making me tired (*why*), but I need to source good drinking water (*what*) because our tap supply is contaminated (*why*)."

Tactics are the *how*—the operational elements or specific actions that you take within the framework provided by your strategy. "I shall buy sparkling water and attractive glasses to drink it from."

Here's another example. If a business strategy is to increase brand awareness, tactics could include specific marketing campaigns, social media engagement plans, and public relations efforts. Each of these tactics should be designed to directly boost brand visibility, aligning with the strategic goal.

For a personal strategy focused on health improvement, tactics might involve specific dietary changes, a scheduled exercise regimen, and regular health check-ups. Each of these directly contributes to improving health, in line with the strategic intent.

Regularly assess whether your tactics are effectively contributing to your strategy. This involves looking at outcomes and determining if they are moving you closer to your strategic goals.

Be prepared to adapt or change tactics that are not effectively aligned with your strategy. Flexibility in tactical execution is key to responding to challenges or changing circumstances.

Your action plan should integrate tactics and strategy in a coherent manner. The tactics should collectively form a pattern that is recognizable as leading towards the strategic objectives.

Make sure you allocate resources (time, money, effort) to tactics in a manner that reflects their importance and contribution to the strategy.

If you're working within a team, it's important that everyone understands how their tasks (tactics) contribute to the larger goals (strategy). Clear communication regarding this alignment is crucial because it fosters a sense of purpose and direction for everyone involved.

When you align your tactics with your strategy you ensure that every action you take is purposeful and contributes to achieving the larger goals. It's about creating a coherent and integrated approach where tactics are not isolated actions but are part of a well-orchestrated plan leading towards strategic success. What we need to do now is to drill down into what tactics look like.

Tactics must be realistic and achievable

Tactics must be realistic and achievable if your planning and execution is to be effective.

Realistic tactics

Realistic tactics are those that can be feasibly executed within the constraints of your current resources, capabilities, and circumstances. They take into account the practical aspects of your situation, including time, finances, skills, and other available resources.

You need to set achievable targets or actions that are challenging, yet attainable. Unrealistic tactics can lead to frustration, burnout, or disengagement, as they set you up for failure right from the start.

Take this example. If you are aiming for a career advancement, a realistic tactic might be to take on additional responsibilities in your current role before seeking a promotion. An unrealistic tactic might be aiming for a high-level position without the necessary experience or qualifications.

Achievable tactics

Achievable tactics are designed with success in mind. They are within the realm of your abilities and resources. This does not mean they can't be challenging, but they should be within a range that you can reasonably expect to accomplish.

There is an added benefit to designing achievable tactics. You will build your confidence and maintain your motivation if you can successfully achieve your targets or perform the actions. It provides a sense of progress and achievement, crucial for long-term engagement with your goals.

Take this example. If your goal is to get fit and you're new to exercise, an achievable tactic might be starting with a 20-minute daily workout. Being new to exercise, you may find immediately aiming for an hour-long intense regimen is unachievable, resulting in you getting demoralized and abandoning your goal.

Stretch but don't snap

While tactics should push you beyond your comfort zone, they shouldn't be so far out of reach that they become demoralizing. The balance is in stretching your abilities without snapping your capacity or resources.

Tactics should allow for incremental progression. As you develop skills and gather more resources, you can adjust your tactics to become more challenging.

Adaptability

Realistic and achievable tactics are not set in stone. You should regularly reassess and adjust them based on your progress, learning, and any changes in circumstances.

Be prepared to modify your tactics if they are proving to be unrealistic or unachievable, or if your situation changes.

Importance of planning and research

Spend time researching and planning to determine what is realistic and achievable. This might involve looking at past experiences, seeking advice, or considering current trends and data.

When you ensure that tactics are realistic and achievable, you are setting yourself up for success. It involves thoughtful planning and an honest assessment of your capabilities and resources. This approach leads to sustainable progress and helps you maintain your motivation and confidence, all of which are crucial for achieving your long-term goals. But for this to work, it's important to implement your tactics consistently.

Consistency and Routine in tactics

Consistency and routine help establish a steady rhythm of action that contributes to the success of your strategies. The two things are slightly different.

Consistent tactics are those that you implement regularly and reliably. For example, if your goal is "to improve my physical fitness" and your tactic is "going to the gym," consistency might mean adhering to a workout schedule of 30 minutes a day, five days a week, without significant gaps. Turning up every day is consistent behavior.

Consistency in action is key to building momentum towards your goal. By consistently applying your tactics, you gradually develop habits that align with your goals. Habits, once established, require less conscious effort to maintain.

Consistency allows for more predictable outcomes. When actions are repeated regularly, their effects become more apparent and measurable.

Routine tactics

Routine tactics are integrated into your daily or weekly routines. They become part of your regular schedule, making it more likely that you'll stick to them. For example, if your goal is to write a book, a routine tactic could involve setting aside two hours for writing every morning before starting your day's usual activities.

A routine provides structure and efficiency. When a tactic becomes part of your routine, you spend less time deciding whether to do it and more time actually doing it. Over time, as the tactic becomes routine, the initial resistance or procrastination often associated with new tasks diminishes.

Benefits of consistency and routine

Consistent and routine actions build momentum. They make it easier to track and measure progress because you are doing things according to a pattern. That helps you identify what's working and what's not.

Each step, no matter how small, adds up over time, contributing significantly to achieving your goals and you can clearly see how your actions contribute to your goals.

While consistency and routine are important, they should be balanced with flexibility. You can allow for quicker adjustments and improvements by working in a methodical manner, so be prepared to adjust your tactics if they are no longer serving your goal, or if changes in your circumstances require it.

Regularly review your routines to ensure they remain aligned with your goals and strategies. Adjust as necessary while maintaining the overall consistency of action.

Examples of strategies and tactics to reach goals

So, you can see how this works in practice, I'm going to show you what strategies and tactics might be employed in three common situations.

Goal: to launch a business

Strategy
The overall strategy might be to establish a competitive presence in a specific market within the first year.

Tactics
» Conduct market research to identify target customer needs and preferences.
» Develop a unique product or service offering based on this research.
» Create a robust marketing plan that includes social media marketing, content marketing, and local community engagement.
» Network with industry professionals and potential clients.

Process
Start with market research to inform product development, followed by marketing efforts to build brand awareness and networking to establish business relationships.

Goal: to write a book

Strategy

The strategy could be to complete a manuscript for a novel within a specified time-frame, say one year, and get it ready for publication.

Tactics

» Set a daily or weekly writing goal (e.g. word count or number of pages).

» Dedicate specific hours each day to writing.

» Periodically review and revise chapters.

» Engage with a writing group or a book coach for feedback and support.

» Once the manuscript is publish-ready, research and reach out to potential publishers, or explore self-publishing options.

Process

Consistently dedicate time to writing and revising, while seeking feedback. Note how after completing the manuscript, the focus shifts to getting it published.

Goal: to achieve fitness goals

Strategy

The strategy might be to improve overall fitness, measured by specific indicators such as weight, muscle tone, or cardiovascular health, over six months.

Tactics

» Develop a regular exercise routine that includes a mix of cardio, strength training, and flexibility exercises.

» Set a schedule for workouts, gradually increasing intensity and duration.

» Monitor diet and nutrition, possibly with the help of a nutritionist or diet app.

» Track progress through regular fitness assessments or using a fitness tracker.

Process

Start with a manageable workout routine and a balanced diet, gradually intensifying the workouts. Regularly track progress and adjust the routine as needed.

Do you see how, in each of these examples, the strategies provide the overall direction and end-goals, while the tactics are the specific actions taken to realize these strategies? The process involves the practical implementation of these tactics, monitoring progress, and making adjustments as needed. If you adopt this approach, you are making sure each step you take is purposeful and contributes effectively towards your larger strategic goals.

Talking of your larger strategic goals, it's time to start thinking about the practical application of all this learning to your actual Black Dots.

Craft strategies and tactics to tackle your Black Dots

I have created a tool, the "Crafting Strategies and Tactics Worksheet," that you can find at the beginning of the next section. Before you rush to print that off, I am going to walk you through the thinking you need to do before you fill in the worksheet.

Earlier in the book, you identified your Black Dots. If you need to, reread your Black Dot map so that what you need to tackle is at the front of your mind.

First, let's address why I am inviting you to develop your strategies and tactics. Crafting a comprehensive strategy lays the groundwork for achieving your goals and commitments to tackle your Black Dots.

It's important to create a comprehensive strategy so that you can understand the big picture of what you need to do. You are going to need to define your vision, and your end-goals. What are you aiming to achieve in the long run? This vision should align with your core values and the essence of your Black Dot journey.

Evaluate where you currently stand in relation to your goals. This assessment includes understanding your strengths, weaknesses, opportunities, and potential challenges.

Break down your vision into specific, measurable objectives. These objectives should be clear and concise, providing a direct path towards your larger vision. Determine the order of priority for these objectives. Some goals may be foundational and need to be achieved before others can be tackled.

Now you are going to work out an Actionable Plan. For each objective, develop strategies that outline how you plan to achieve them. These strategies should consider the most effective methods and approaches given your resources and constraints.

Then, break down each strategy into specific tactics or actions. These should be practical, actionable steps that you can take to advance each strategy.

Identify what resources you will need for each aspect of your strategy. These may be time, money, information, skills, and other physical or intangible assets.

Plan how you are going to optimize the use of these resources. Efficient resource management is key to the successful implementation of your strategy.

While your strategy should be comprehensive, it also needs to be flexible. Be prepared to adapt and modify your plan as you progress and as circumstances change.

Include contingency plans for potential obstacles or unexpected changes.

Establish mechanisms for tracking progress towards each objective. This could involve regular reviews, checkpoints, or specific metrics to assess performance.

Use the insights gained from monitoring to make informed adjustments to your strategy and tactics.

If your journey involves others, communicate your strategy clearly to all stakeholders. Their buy-in and support can be crucial.

Create a support network that aligns with and supports your strategic goals. This network can provide motivation, resources, and different perspectives.

This is all to show you that in your Black Dot journey, crafting a comprehensive strategy is about taking a holistic view of your goals and creating a detailed, actionable plan to achieve them. It's a process that combines careful planning, resource management, adaptability, and continuous monitoring. This strategic approach ensures that every step you take is purposeful and directly contributes to the realization of your goals.

The Crafting Strategies and Tactics Worksheet

The "Crafting Strategies and Tactics Worksheet" is a practical tool designed to assist you in developing effective strategies and tactics for overcoming your Black Dots—the challenges or obstacles you face.

This worksheet is designed to guide you through the process, from crafting a vision to tracking progress and making necessary adjustments. You can also download a copy of this tool from www.theblackdotphilosophy.com

Fill out each section thoughtfully, considering the long-term impact of your actions and each aspect of your personal growth plan.

Vision and Alignment
- Define your overarching vision for overcoming your Black Dots
- Ensure this vision aligns with your core values and your journey's essence.

Current State Assessment
- Evaluate your current position in relation to your goals
- Conduct a SWOT analysis (Strengths, Weaknesses, Opportunities, Threats).

Objective Setting
- Break down your vision into specific, measurable objectives
- Prioritize these objectives based on foundational importance and feasibility.

Actionable Plan Development
- For each objective, devise comprehensive strategies detailing your approach
- Break down each strategy into specific, practical, and actionable tactics.

Resource Identification
- List the resources needed for each strategy, such as time, money, skills
- Plan for the efficient utilization of these resources.

Flexibility and Adaptability
- Keep your strategies adaptable for unforeseen circumstances
- Develop contingency plans for potential obstacles.

Progress Tracking and Review
- Set up regular reviews and checkpoints to track progress
- Establish specific metrics for performance assessment.

Insights and Adjustments
- Use progress insights to make informed adjustments to strategies and tactics
- Revisit and update this worksheet as you progress in your Black Dot journey.

You can use this worksheet to systematically fill in your own strategies and tactics for dealing with your Black Dots. This structured approach will help you in effectively planning and executing your actions towards achieving your goals.

Key components of the worksheet

Identification of Black Dots
Start by listing down the black dots or challenges you are currently facing. These could be personal, professional, health-related, or any other areas of concern.

Provide details about each Black Dot. What makes it a challenge? How does it impact you?

Goal-setting
For each identified black dot, define a goal that represents overcoming or addressing this challenge. Remember that each goal must be worded in such a way as to make it specific, measurable, achievable, relevant, and time-bound (SMART).

Strategy development

For each goal, outline strategies that could effectively lead to overcoming your Black Dots. Strategies should provide a broad approach or method for tackling these challenges.

Be open to using different types of strategies. Some might tackle the problem directly while others seek to change your mindset about your Black Dot.

Tactics identification

Under each strategy, list the specific tactics or actions you will take. These should be concrete steps that can be acted upon.

Include details such as when you will take these actions, who is responsible (if others are involved), and any resources required.

Resources assessment

Determine what resources are needed to carry out each tactic. This might include time, money, information, skills, or other resources.

If you currently don't have these resources, plan how you will acquire them.

Timeline creation

Establish a timeline for each tactic. (See the Resources Library at the end of the book for a template.) When will you start? What are the deadlines for completion? Include regular points in time to review progress on each tactic. Weekly? Monthly? On what milestones?

Monitoring and adjustment

Decide how you will monitor progress for each tactic. What indicators will you use to assess whether you are on track?

Be prepared to adjust your tactics if they are not proving effective or if circumstances change.

Reflection and learning

You've noted down on your Timeline the points at which you will reflect on what you're learning through this process. At those points, ask yourself, what insights are you gaining? How are these challenges shaping your growth?

Use your reflections and learning to adapt your strategies and tactics over time.

Once you have established clear goals and the strategies and tactics you need to adopt to reach them, you need to create an action plan to carry out your commitments.

Create an Action Plan

An effective action plan is a detailed guide designed to help you achieve your goals and commitments. I am going to show you what you need to have in place to create your plan. If you need to remind yourself how to make your goals, strategies, and tactics in detail, refer to the earlier sections.

Core elements of an effective Action Plan

The action plan we have in mind here is not a simple To Do list. It brings together all the work you have already done to define your purpose, goals, strategies, and tactics.

It incorporates a timeline, and it identifies what resources and tools you will need.

Once you have identified your actions, you may need to assign to others ownership or responsibility for carrying them out. That information goes into your action plan, along with mechanisms for tracking your progress and evaluating the impact of change.

Your Action Plan includes contingency plans and reminders to engage in regular reflective practice.

How to develop your Action Plan

Clear objectives

Make a note at the top of your plan of your goals expressed as clear, specific objectives. What exactly do you want to achieve? These should align with your purpose and be as precise as possible.

Ensure that your goals are measurable, so you can track your progress and know when you have achieved them.

On your plan, deal with one goal at a time using the following prompts to drill down to the specific actions that need to be taken to achieve the goal.

Strategy

Include a reminder of the strategies you have adopted to reach your goal.

Tactics

Include a reminder of the tactics you have adopted to execute your strategy.

Actions

Many of your tactics may also be actions or tasks. However, if a tactic entails carrying out two or more different actions to perform it, then break the tactic down into the component actions. Ensure that your tactic or action, whichever is the smallest unit of action, is actionable and practical considering your resources and constraints.

Assigning responsibilities and roles

If your plan involves others, clearly define responsibilities and roles. Who is responsible for what? Ensure everyone involved understands their tasks and commitments.

For personal goals that affect no one else, take ownership of each tactic, action, or task. Remind yourself that you are responsible for executing the plan.

Timeline

Draw a clear timeline with deadlines for each action or milestone. This helps keep you on track and provides a sense of urgency. (While it's important to stick to your timeline, also be prepared to adjust it as needed based on your progress and any unforeseen circumstances.)

Resources and tools

Identify what resources (such as time, money, information, and tools) you need for each tactic. Plan how you will acquire or access these resources. What action do you need to take? Note it down under the Actions part of your plan.

Consider what tools or technology can aid in the implementation of your plan. This might include project management software, educational materials, or specialized equipment. Do you need to acquire them? Are there any other associated actions? Note them down.

Monitoring and evaluation

Include a system for tracking your progress. How will you measure success for each tactic and overall strategy?

Plan for regular reviews of your progress against the action plan. Schedule them. This allows you to make adjustments as needed and address any challenges.

Contingency plans

Consider potential obstacles or challenges that might arise and plan for how you will address them. What assumptions might you have made that may not be true? What circumstances could you predict might change that would impact your plans?

Have contingency plans in case primary strategies or tactics do not work out as expected.

Reflective practice

Incorporate periods for reflective practice into your plan. Schedule thinking time for yourself so you can reflect on what is working, what is not, and why. Use these insights to adapt and improve your approach.

....

Think about your own Black Dot journey

We have explored the dynamic between strategies and tactics and how these concepts play a crucial role in Black Dot success. We've also looked at the importance of planning in the Black Dot journey.

To help you embed the Philosophy into your own outlook, I suggest you do this:

- Define a clear strategy for your Black Dot challenge
- List tactical maneuvers to execute your strategy effectively
- Reflect on the role of planning and its impact on overcoming obstacles
- Share your strategy and tactics for your specific Black Dot challenge
- Describe how having a well-defined plan empowers you to tackle challenges.

NOTES

STEP 5

MAINTAIN YOUR MOMENTUM

This next chapter is really important! As you will see, accountability and responsibility play a huge role in your ability to build upon your Black Dot process and the implementation of your strategies and tactics in order to overcome obstacles and challenges and realize your full potential as you achieve the kind unimaginable results you deserve.

Your journey requires resilience and adaptability. You will face challenges in pursuit of your goals, and sometimes the changes you face on your journey can be life-changing. Sometimes they seem to appear out of nowhere.

Thankfully, I had acquired a tremendous amount of resiliency and adaptability over the years thanks to The Black Dot Philosophy in both my personal and professional life. I had no idea how these attributes would play such a significant role later in my life when I would come face to face with a massive Black adopt in the summer of 2014.

As you know, my son decided to pursue his education in Santa Barbara, California. So here I am, working and living just outside of Cleveland, Ohio, while he is doing his homework at the beach in sunny Southern California. When he told me that he wanted to go to college in California, I immediately picked up the phone and called the company to let them know that I wanted to get back to Southern California should an opportunity arise in the near future. It paid off two years later when I got a call offering me the Los Angeles General Office.

I accepted even though the General Office was reconfigured and some of the territory was given to another Managing Partner who had recently become the Managing Partner in Glendale and Pasadena, which was previously part of the Los Angeles office. At this point in my life and career it really didn't matter because I wanted to get back home in the worst way now that my son was back.

I minimized that Black Dot by eliminating the situation from my mind as it was out of my control, and I went right to work using the Black Dot Philosophy to create a game plan to grow the General Office and went to work.

Additionally, I was raised and lived most of my life in the L.A. area, and I was thrilled to be back home after moving four times over the last 15 years. Not to mention I could see my son as often as we could make the time to get together, which was a lot.

Fast forward to June 2014. I was living with my girlfriend at that time in Marina del Rey. Life was good, and I was very happy. In fact, my son was graduating and getting his degree in communications from UCSB that June, and so I took my father and a close friend of mine who was like Tyler's uncle, and we met up with Tyler's siblings and his mother who were all there for his graduation. It was an exciting time, and I was so proud watching him get his diploma. Unfortunately, by the end of that weekend, I wasn't feeling that good, and by the time I got home that Sunday night, I had a fever and I also had what looked like a hernia on the left side of my abdomen.

The following day, I decided that I needed to go to the emergency hospital at UCLA, close to where I was living. When I was being examined, the nurse commented on how big my hernia was and that it was good I decided to come in that day. I was kind of relieved that she said that, as I wasn't so sure that's what it was.

I was fully examined that day and had a series of tests. My worst fear came to fruition when I was told that my "hernia" wasn't really a hernia. Instead, it was a swollen lymph gland. My temperature went up as the day progressed, along with a blistering headache, and overall, I felt horrible. They could not diagnose anything while I was there, and so they sent me home with instructions to see my Internal Medicine Doctor immediately.

When I woke up the next day, my temperature was 104 degrees, my headache would not go away, the bulge in my abdomen was getting bigger, and I had blisters on my skin. I knew this was not anything I had ever experienced, and I got pretty nervous about what kind of medical issue I might potentially be dealing with.

Over the next few days, I had a battery of tests. I was also too sick to go to work. That in itself was a big Black Dot because the two most important times of the year for my company were June and December. June was critically important as it was the end of the recognition year for agents and advisors. So typically, you are working around the clock in June, and there are high expectations from the folks in Manhattan.

I called my direct report and told him I was too ill to work and had no idea what was wrong with me. It was obviously a cause for concern, but because of HIPAA, no one from Corporate could ask questions about my health. I just updated them as to my inability to work. The guilt I felt was overwhelming.

After two weeks of suffering beyond anything I had ever experienced, the doctors still could not identify the problem. I felt helpless and I was extremely discouraged and quite frankly, I really thought that this was the end of my life.

Thankfully, not long after that two-week period of knowing absolutely nothing, I got a call from my doctor. He told me that I needed to see a particular doctor at the Infectious Disease Center at UCLA. He said that the doctor I would be seeing was going to share the results of a very specific test I was finally given a few days before and that I needed to be there at 3:00.

Needless to say, I was pretty freaked out, especially since all of my symptoms, along with some new ones, were getting worse by the day. I honestly felt like I was dying, and the next day I found out that I actually was well on my way to an early death! The doctor at the Infectious Disease Center told me that they did an HIV test on me that originally came back negative. He said that they ended up giving me another test that was more comprehensive because they had eliminated every disease or infection up to that point. He went on to say that this new and more detailed test did, in fact, show that I had acquired HIV.

Honestly, if it weren't for the Black Dot Philosophy, I am not sure that I would have been able to handle the diagnosis, especially since I witnessed my sister deteriorate and ultimately pass away from the AIDS virus at age 30. Using the Black Dot to put it all in perspective and then create a game plan to manage my emotions was a tremendous help.

The doctor explained that they didn't have a cure yet but that they had medication that would ultimately not only make me better but over a very short period of time the HIV would be totally undetectable and I could have a completely normal life by just taking one pill a day.

Within the next couple of weeks, I felt perfectly fine, and soon thereafter the HIV was completely undetectable and has been that way for the last ten years. I learned that if I took a normal HIV test, I would pass and that it was virtually impossible to spread the virus, including unprotected sex. There has not been a recorded situation where someone who was undetectable actually infected another person through any kind of contact, including unprotected sex. As of June

2024, I am still completely undetectable and have lived a very normal and healthy life!

Unfortunately, when it was diagnosed, I was told that I had contracted it very recently. Well, other than my girlfriend at that time, there wasn't a situation where I could have gotten it from anyone else. He confirmed that I got it from my girlfriend and that she was obviously unaware that she was a carrier of the virus. I later found out that she got it from her former husband, who apparently cheated on her while they were married, and I will leave it there. We broke up the following year, but I stayed in contact with her, and she is also very healthy and undetectable today.

When I was diagnosed, I decided that I was only going to tell my son and a couple of close friends. So when I was back on my feet in early July, I went back to work and pretended I had a bad virus and I fully recovered. We went on to have a great year, but it took its toll on me. In retrospect, I should have taken a disability leave of absence for a few months so I could get my head around the situation. Instead, I buried it in my mind and focused on my work. Not the best approach, but it worked in the short term.

This was where my years of using the Black Dot to strengthen my resiliency paid off, as I was able to bounce back quickly and get back to work like nothing happened. On the other hand, I kept it to myself, and that was a big mistake in retrospect. I felt like damaged goods, didn't date, and even thought that I would never have an intimate relationship with a woman again. It's also painful to live with a secret like this, and it didn't have to be that way.

I eventually went public through social media five years later and after I had retired. I was on a three-month vacation in Italy, and I made a video on the fifth anniversary of contracting the virus, and it was also my fifth anniversary of being completely undetectable. The outpouring of love from family and friends was overwhelming. I felt like me again, and the pain of keeping it a secret disappeared!

Examples of notable figures who have successfully maintained their momentum include:

1. **David Goggins**: Former Navy SEAL and ultra-endurance athlete known for his mental toughness and commitment to personal growth.
2. **Brené Brown**: Research professor and author, recognized for her work on vulnerability and leadership.
3. **Nelson Mandela**: Former President of South Africa, known for his resilience and leadership in ending apartheid and uniting a divided nation.
4. **Alex Honnold:** Rock climber known for his free solo ascents, requiring immense discipline and mental focus.
5. **Simone Biles**: Olympic gymnast whose dedication and mental strength are exemplary for maintaining momentum.

Accountability and personal responsibility

Now you know what your Black Dots are, what your purpose in life is, what goals to tackle your Black Dots you need to set that are aligned with your purpose, what strategies and tactics you will employ to reach those goals, we need to think about how you are going to sustain your energy and commitment to achieving those goals.

We have already talked about the importance of declaring your goals when you have set them. Now we are going to dig a little deeper into the concepts of Accountability and Personal Responsibility.

Accountability and a sense of personal responsibility play a crucial role in your commitment to and achievement of goals. Taking responsibility for one's own commitments is a fundamental driver in achieving your goals and personal growth. It involves acknowledging and accepting your role in your own success or failure.

While public accountability provides an external motivation and support system, personal responsibility empowers and drives you from within. Together, these elements create a robust framework for successfully your achieving goals.

Accountability, whether to oneself or others, enhances the level of your commitment to a goal. Knowing that you are answerable for your actions and progress—even if only you know of your intent—adds a layer of seriousness and urgency to your endeavors.

For many, the knowledge that someone else is aware of, and interested in, their progress can be a powerful motivator. This can come from a mentor, coach, peer group, or even a broader audience.

Personal responsibility involves taking ownership of your goals and the actions required to achieve them. It's about acknowledging that you are the primary driver of your success.

Embracing personal responsibility is empowering. It shifts your mindset from external reliance to internal drive, reinforcing the belief that you have control over your actions and outcomes.

Interplay of Accountability and Responsibility

While accountability involves external checks and support, personal responsibility is about internal commitment. Together, they create a powerful combination that can significantly boost the likelihood of achieving goals.

Finding the right balance between external accountability and internal responsibility is key. Too much reliance on external accountability can diminish self-motivation, while too little may lead to a lack of discipline. Be prepared to adjust your accountability systems as needed. What works initially may need to be adapted as you progress towards your goal or as your circumstances change.

Strategies for building Accountability

Establish relationships with accountability partners who can check in on your progress.

Make public declarations of your goals to create a sense of accountability to others.

Set up a system of regular reporting on your progress, whether it's through social media updates, blog posts, or group meetings.

Strategies for cultivating Personal Responsibility

Regularly engage in self-reflection to assess your progress and the effectiveness of your actions.

Develop and adhere to personal standards of performance that align with your goals.

Strengthen your self-discipline practices. This might include maintaining consistent work schedules, setting, and adhering to, deadlines, and resisting distractions.

How to embrace and uphold Accountability and Responsibility

Take Ownership of actions and decisions

Taking responsibility means acknowledging that you are in control of your actions and decisions. It's understanding that your progress towards your goals is largely dependent on the choices you make each day.

This ownership is empowering. It shifts the focus from external factors to internal control, highlighting that you have the power to influence your own life's trajectory.

Recognize the impact of choices

Understand that each decision or action has consequences that impact your goal pursuit. Taking responsibility involves being mindful of these consequences and making choices that align with your commitments.

When outcomes are not as expected, instead of blaming someone else, take responsibility for your own decision. Learn from the experience and use these lessons to inform future decisions.

Commitment to self-improvement

Embrace the commitment to continually learn and grow. This means actively seeking opportunities for self-improvement and personal development.

Be willing to adapt and change strategies as needed. Taking responsibility includes being flexible and responsive to new information and experiences.

Exercise self-discipline and practice consistency

Uphold a disciplined approach to your commitments. Consistent effort, even in small doses, is key to making progress towards your goals.

Develop routines and habits that support your goals. These practices help in maintaining a steady course of action.

Handle setbacks with resilience

Accept that setbacks and challenges are part of the journey. Taking responsibility means facing these challenges head-on and working through them, rather than giving up.

Cultivate resilience by viewing setbacks as opportunities for growth and learning, rather than as insurmountable obstacles.

Seek and utilize feedback

Actively seek and be open to feedback, whether from mentors, peers, or through self-reflection. Constructive feedback is a valuable tool for growth and improvement.

Take responsibility for implementing necessary changes based on the feedback you receive. It's about acting on what you learn.

Self-motivation and self-encouragement

Cultivate your sense of drive and motivation. Encourage yourself through affirmations, celebrating small wins, and reminding yourself of the larger purpose behind your goals.

Hold yourself accountable

Regularly review your progress towards your goals. Be honest with yourself about your efforts and achievements.

If you find yourself off track, take responsibility to adjust your course of action.

Taking responsibility for your own commitments is about recognizing and embracing your power to influence your life's direction. It involves a conscious effort to make choices that align with your goals, to learn from experiences, and to maintain a disciplined and resilient approach towards achieving your objectives.

As you get underway, implementing your strategies and tactics to achieve your goals, you will need to know how to keep going. In the next section, I'm going to show you the need for different approaches and mindsets at various stages of the "Commitment Continuum."

Nurturing Commitment Over Time

The Commitment Continuum

We are going to explore the evolution of commitment; from the initial enthusiasm you'll feel for getting started to the long-term dedication you need to achieve your goals. Commitment is not static; it changes and develops over time, requiring you to adopt different approaches, and to vary your mindset, at various stages.

Here's how commitment typically evolves.

Initial enthusiasm

When you first make a commitment, there's often a surge of excitement and energy. This initial enthusiasm is driven by the novelty of the goal and the anticipation of change or achievement.

Leverage momentum

Use this initial burst of energy to set up structures and plans that will support your goal. This might include establishing routines, making necessary preparations, or gathering resources.

Encountering challenges

As the initial excitement wanes, you may encounter challenges or obstacles that test your commitment. This is a normal and expected part of any journey towards a significant goal.

Building resilience

Develop strategies to deal with these challenges. This might include seeking support, learning new skills, or adjusting your approach.

Sustained effort and routine

Integrate your goals as much as you can into your daily life. Over time, working towards your goal should become part of your regular routine. The key here is to maintain a consistent effort and not lose sight of your commitment.

Focus on building habits that align with your commitment. The more ingrained these habits become, the less effort it will take to sustain them.

Renew motivation

To keep your commitment strong, actively seek new sources of motivation and inspiration. This could be through reading, engaging with a community, or reflecting on the progress you've made. Share your experiences and insights with others. This not only helps in solidifying your own commitment but can also inspire and guide others in their journeys.

Celebrate milestones

Regularly celebrate your achievements, no matter how small. These celebrations can reignite your enthusiasm and motivation.

Seek deeper understanding

As time progresses, reflect on what you've learned about yourself and your goals. Use these insights to refine and possibly redefine your commitment.

Adapt

Be open to adapting your goals as you grow and as circumstances change. Flexibility is crucial for long-term success.

Embed in your identity

Eventually, your commitment becomes a part of who you are. It's no longer just something you do; it's a part of your identity. Even when the initial goal is achieved, the commitment often continues in some form, whether it's through setting new goals, mentoring others, or continuing practices that have become meaningful.

Legacy

Consider the broader impact of your commitment. How does it affect others? What kind of legacy does it create?

The "Commitment Continuum" is about understanding and navigating the evolving nature of commitment. It's about leveraging your initial enthusiasm, overcoming challenges, sustaining your effort, renewing your motivation, and ultimately embedding the commitment into your very sense of identity. This journey requires resilience and adaptability, and for you to make a continuous reconnection with the underlying purpose of your commitment.

Practical tips to maintain and deepen your commitment

You will face challenges in pursuit of your goal and so it is essential that you know how to maintain and deepen your commitment.

Revisit and reinforce your Why

Remember your purpose. Regularly remind yourself why you made the commitment in the first place. Reconnecting with the underlying reasons for your goal can reignite your motivation.

Keep a clear vision of what success looks like and the benefits it will bring. This can be a powerful motivator to keep pushing forward.

Set realistic expectations

Understand that challenges and setbacks are normal and part of the process. Acknowledge that the path to your goal is not easy. Setting realistic expectations helps in maintaining a balanced perspective.

Make goals manageable

Break down your larger goals into smaller, manageable tasks. Achieving these smaller goals can boost confidence and motivation.

Develop a support system

Lean on friends, family, mentors, or peer groups for support. They can offer encouragement, advice, and a different perspective.

Engage with communities that share similar goals. Being part of a group can provide a sense of solidarity and additional motivation.

Cultivate resilience

View setbacks as learning opportunities. Analyze what went wrong and what can be done differently next time.

Be willing to adapt your approach if something is not working. Flexibility is key to overcoming challenges.

Maintain discipline and consistency:

Stick to your routines and continue to foster habits that support your goals. Consistency in action, even when it's challenging, is crucial for long-term success.

Schedule regular reviews of your progress. This can help keep you on track and make necessary adjustments.

Engage in positive self-talk

Practice positive self-talk. Encourage yourself with affirmations and remind yourself of your capabilities and past successes. Actively challenge and reframe negative thoughts or doubts that may arise.

Seek inspiration and learning

Read or listen to stories of people who have overcome similar challenges. Learning from others' experiences can provide valuable insights and inspiration.

Embrace a mindset of continuous learning. Whether it's acquiring new skills or gaining new knowledge, this can enhance your ability to meet challenges.

Celebrate progress

Celebrate your achievements, no matter how small. Recognizing progress is important for maintaining motivation and a sense of accomplishment.

Mindfulness and stress management

Engage in mindfulness exercises such as meditation or yoga. These practices can help manage stress and maintain emotional balance.

Regular physical activity can also be an effective way to manage stress and maintain a healthy state of mind.

Journaling and reflection

Keep a journal of your journey. Writing about your experiences, challenges, and feelings can provide clarity and a sense of progress.

By employing these strategies, you can maintain and deepen your commitment even when challenges arise. It's about staying connected to your purpose, being realistic and flexible, cultivating support networks, and continuously fostering resilience and self-encouragement.

Remember, commitment is a dynamic process that evolves and deepens over time, especially through the trials and triumphs of your journey. The dynamic nature of the process calls for you to be adaptable especially when faced with changing circumstances.

Adaptability

The ability to adapt ensures that your commitments remain relevant, achievable, and aligned with your goals and values, even as situations evolve.

How Adaptability supports your commitment

The inevitability of Change

Expect change. It's important to recognize that change is an inevitable part of life. Whether these changes are personal, professional, or societal, they can impact the feasibility and relevance of your commitments.

Proactive adaptation

Where possible, try to anticipate potential changes and plan for them in advance. This proactive approach can make the adaptation process smoother.

Embrace a dynamic mindset

Cultivate a mindset that is open to change and new possibilities. This openness can make adapting to new circumstances less daunting.

Cultivate resilience

Part of being adaptable is being resilient. Develop the ability to bounce back from setbacks and adjust your course as necessary. Be willing to adapt your approach if something is not working.

Recognize when something is not working

Prepare to be flexible. Flexibility is key to overcoming challenges. Being adaptable means allowing your goals and commitments to evolve as circumstances change. Clinging too rigidly to the original form of a commitment can lead to frustration or failure if circumstances no longer support it.

Adapt strategies, not abandon your goals

When faced with new challenges or changes, consider modifying your strategies or methods rather than abandoning your goals altogether. Look for alternative paths to achieve the same end. Regularly assess your commitment strategies to ensure they are still effective under the new circumstances.

Make small adjustments

Sometimes, small, incremental adjustments are more effective than major overhauls in response to change.

Maintain your core values

While your strategies and goals might change, ensure they still align with your core values. Adaptability should not mean compromising on what is fundamentally important to you.

Revisit your Why

In times of change, revisit the reasons behind your commitment. This can help realign your adapted goals with your core values and purpose.

Learn and grow from change

Changes often bring new insights and perspectives. Embrace these as opportunities for learning and growth. Use the new knowledge and experiences gained from dealing with changes to enhance and refine your commitment.

Seek support and feedback

During times of change, seek advice and feedback from mentors, peers, or professionals. They can provide different perspectives and advice on adapting your commitments. Rely on your support network for encouragement and motivation as you navigate through changes.

When the going gets too rough, adaptability is your friend. Maintain the fluidity and flexibility to adjust your goals and methods in response to changing circumstances while staying true to your core values and overarching purpose. Adaptability involves being open to learning, willing to seek support, and capable of making strategic adjustments. This dynamic approach ensures that your commitments remain relevant, realistic, and aligned with your personal growth and evolving life situation.

Impact of Change on your Declarations

Adjusting your commitment declarations as needed is an essential part of ensuring that your goals remain relevant and achievable. Here are some strategies to revise and update your commitment declarations:

Review your Commitments regularly

Set regular intervals (monthly, quarterly, etc.) to review your commitment declarations. Assess whether they still align with your current circumstances, values, and long-term objectives.

Consider any significant changes in your life, such as shifts in personal priorities, professional developments, or new challenges and opportunities that have arisen.

Be flexible

Cultivate an attitude of flexibility. Be open to modifying your goals, or, preferably, the strategies you employ to reach them unless the goal has truly become redundant, as your situation and understanding evolve.

Make incremental adjustments

Instead of completely overhauling your commitments, consider making incremental adjustments that better align with your current context.

Revisit your Why

Revisit the underlying reasons why you made the commitment in the first place. Ensure that your adjusted declaration still resonates with these core motivations.

Align with your current values

Check that your revised commitments are still in alignment with your current values and life purpose.

Seeking feedback and advice

Talk to mentors, peers, or other trusted individuals about your proposed adjustments. They can provide valuable perspectives and feedback.

Engage with supportive communities. If you're part of any group or community related to your goals, discuss your thoughts on adjustments with them.

Redrafting your Declaration

Update the Language of your commitment declaration to reflect any changes. Use clear, positive, and assertive language. Ensure your revised commitment is still SMART; Specific, Measurable, Achievable, Relevant, and Time-bound.

Visualizing the adjusted outcome

Spend time visualizing the outcomes of your adjusted commitment. How will achieving these revised goals make you feel?

Emotional connection

Ensure that the revised goals still evoke a strong emotional connection, as this is key to maintaining motivation.

Re-declaration

If your original declaration was public, consider re-declaring your adjusted commitment. This reaffirms your dedication and maintains accountability.

Even if the declaration is private, reaffirming your commitment to yourself is equally important.

Plan for implementation

Outline actionable steps and strategies to achieve your revised goals. Consider any new resources or support you might need.

Set a new timeline or modify existing deadlines to accommodate the changes.

Continued monitoring and adaptation

Continue to monitor your progress towards the revised goals. Be prepared for further adjustments as necessary.

Learn from experience

Use the insights gained from this process of adjustment to inform future goal-setting and commitment practices.

By following these strategies, you can ensure that your commitment declarations remain dynamic and responsive to your evolving life circumstances, enhancing their relevance and the likelihood of successful achievement.

Supportive Environments

We've mentioned the need to surround yourself with people who support your goals, several times. Here we are going to go a little deeper and see why it is not just beneficial but often crucial for success.

Enhanced motivation and energy

Encouragement from others can serve as a powerful form of positive reinforcement, boosting your motivation and drive to pursue your goals.

Support from others can provide the emotional uplift needed to continue in times of challenge or when motivation wanes.

Accountability and responsibility

A supportive environment often includes elements of accountability. Knowing that others are rooting for your success and might ask about your progress can help you stay committed.

Feeling a sense of responsibility towards those who support you can also be a motivating factor, driving you to fulfill your commitments.

Wisdom and diverse perspectives

Supportive individuals can offer valuable insights, advice, and perspectives that you might not have considered. This can be especially useful in overcoming challenges or when making important decisions.

You can learn from others. The experiences and knowledge of those in your support network can provide learning opportunities that enrich your journey.

Reduction of stress and anxiety

A supportive environment can act as an emotional buffer against stress and anxiety. Knowing that you have people to turn to can alleviate feelings of being overwhelmed.

Share the burden. Being able to share your concerns, doubts, and challenges with supportive people can lighten the emotional load often associated with pursuing significant goals.

Network of resources

Supportive networks can also provide access to resources, whether it's information, contacts, skills, or even financial support.

A supportive environment often brings about opportunities for collaboration that accelerate progress and open new avenues.

Building confidence and self-efficacy

Encouragement and positive feedback from others can build your confidence and belief in your ability to achieve your goals.

Having a group to celebrate your successes with can reinforce your self-efficacy and satisfaction.

Creating a healthy and nurturing atmosphere

A supportive environment is typically more constructive and less judgmental. It fosters a healthy space for growth and exploration.

Being surrounded by supportive people contributes to your overall emotional well-being. This is crucial for sustained effort and commitment.

Fostering a sense of belonging

Being part of a supportive group provides a sense of belonging and community, which can be inherently fulfilling and motivating.

Sharing your journey with others who are supportive creates a shared experience, enhancing the sense of camaraderie and mutual support.

When you create a supportive and encouraging group around you, you gain motivation, accountability, diverse insights, stress relief, resources, confidence building, and a sense of belonging. All the while, too, you will be giving back to the group because they, too, will be learning from you and your journey.

Such an environment acts as a catalyst for growth and success, making the challenging journey of realizing significant commitments more achievable and enjoyable. I warmly recommend that you actively foster a supportive and encouraging environment because it will significantly enhance the journey towards achieving your goals.

How to create a supportive and encouraging environment

Seek out like-minded individuals

Join groups, clubs, or communities where members share similar interests or goals. This could be a local sports club, a book club, a professional organization, or online forums and social media groups. Participate actively in these groups. Engage in discussions, attend meetings or events, and contribute where you can.

Build a support network

Identify friends, family members, or colleagues who are supportive of your goals. Make an effort to spend more time with them and discuss your aspirations. Be explicit about the kind of support you're seeking, whether it's accountability, advice, or just a listening ear.

Engage in mentorship

Seek a mentor who has experience or expertise in the area of your goal. A mentor can provide guidance, encouragement, and valuable insights.

Alternatively, consider becoming a mentor to someone else. Teaching or guiding others can also reinforce your own commitment and understanding.

Create a positive home environment

Foster a positive atmosphere at home. Surround yourself with motivational quotes, vision boards, or any other visual reminders of your goals.

Discuss your goals with household members and ask for their support and understanding, especially in terms of respecting your time and commitment.

Leverage online tools and platforms

Use online tools and platforms that are designed for goal tracking and community support. Apps such as *MyFitnessPal* for fitness goals, or *Duolingo* for language learning, often have supportive online communities.

Join or create accountability groups on social media where members can share their progress and challenges.

Nurture relationships with positive communication

Practice positive communication with those around you. Share your successes and challenges openly and be supportive of others' goals and achievements.

Listen actively and offer encouragement and constructive feedback to others. This can foster a mutually supportive dynamic.

Collaborate and share resources

Look for opportunities to collaborate with others on similar goals. This could mean joint projects, shared learning experiences, or co-creating a product.

Share resources, be it information, contacts, or tools, with your network and be open to receiving help in return.

Celebrate successes together

Celebrate your milestones and achievements with your support network. Similarly, be enthusiastic about celebrating others' successes.

Recognize and appreciate the role your support network plays in your achievements.

Foster a growth mindset

Encourage a growth mindset within your support network. Embrace challenges, learn from failures, and encourage continuous learning and development.

Practice gratitude

Show appreciation for the support you receive. Gratitude not only strengthens relationships but also reinforces a positive and supportive environment.

By actively engaging in these practices, you can foster a nurturing and supportive environment that is conducive to achieving your goals. This environment will not only support your own journey but can also inspire and encourage others in their pursuits.

The Power of Small Wins

Celebrating small victories along the way plays a vital role in maintaining your motivation and momentum.

Why Small Wins are so impactful

Reinforce progress

Small wins act as visible milestones of progress. They provide tangible evidence that you are moving forward, even if the end goal is still far off.

Each small victory reinforces the actions that led to it. This positive reinforcement encourages the repetition of those beneficial actions.

Boost confidence

Every small win contributes to building self-efficacy—the belief in your ability to achieve your goals. This growing confidence can be crucial in tackling larger and more challenging aspects of your goal.

Celebrating these achievements can help quell self-doubt and reaffirm your capability to meet your commitments.

Maintain motivation

The journey towards significant goals can be long and challenging. Small wins provide continuous motivation and a sense of achievement that keeps the journey exciting and engaging.

Celebrating small victories can reignite enthusiasm, especially during phases where motivation naturally dips.

Break down goals

Recognizing small wins involves breaking down larger goals into smaller, more manageable segments. This makes the process less overwhelming and more approachable.

It encourages a focus on the present, celebrating what has been achieved, rather than always looking at what is yet to be done.

Enhance well-being

Small wins contribute to an overall sense of accomplishment and well-being. They remind you that you are making progress and that your efforts are yielding results.

By focusing on these successes, you can reduce feelings of stress and anxiety associated with pursuing large goals.

Create momentum

Each small win adds to the momentum towards your larger goal. This cumulative effect can be surprisingly powerful over time.

The confidence and motivation gained from small wins can encourage you to tackle new challenges and set higher goals.

Social sharing and support

Sharing your small victories with others can provide social reinforcement and support. It can also inspire others in their own pursuits.

Celebrating small wins together can strengthen the bonds within your support network and foster a culture of encouragement and positivity.

Recognizing and celebrating small wins, no matter how small the victory, is a key strategy in sustaining your journey towards achieving your larger commitments.

....

Think about your own Black Dot journey

So far, we have looked at how to maintain your momentum by developing accountability and taking personal responsibility.

To help you embed the Philosophy into your own outlook, I suggest you do this:

- Set a date for yourself to declare your goals publicly. Decide what you are going to say, and where you are going to say it.
- To strengthen your practice of self-discipline, set your schedule for the next four weeks and set aside 15 minutes at the end of that period to reflect on how well you adhered to it. What distracted you from it? What changes will you make? What worked really well?

NOTES

STEP
6

HARVEST YOUR SUCCESS

Congratulations! You have identified your Black Dots and learned how to tackle them, by identifying your purpose in life, setting goals that align with your purpose to overcome your Black Dots, developing strategies and by working out tactics and creating an action plan.

You have learned how to strengthen and sustain your motivation to stay the course and achieve your goals, by using a mix of personal discipline, private commitment, and public declarations, by creating a supportive environment around you and by deepening your reflective practices of gratitude and visualization.

You understand what touches your emotions and you know how to monitor and adjust your progress. Now you can bring all this learning together to bring new meaning to your life.

Recap of the Black Dot Philosophy

This would be a good moment to review the key principles and takeaways of the Black Dot Philosophy. Let's summarize its transformative approach just to refresh your memory before you put this book down and get to work on your own Black Dots.

Examples of notable figures who have successfully harvested their success include:

1. **Walt Disney**: Pioneer of the American animation industry, whose creativity and innovation led to the creation of one of the most successful entertainment companies in the world.
2. **Bill Gates**: Co-founder of Microsoft, who continues to influence the tech industry and philanthropy.
3. **Steven Spielberg**: Renowned filmmaker who transformed his early passion into a legendary career.
4. **Angela Merkel**: Former Chancellor of Germany, known for her steady leadership and success in navigating complex political landscapes.
5. **Trevor Noah**: Comedian and host of The Daily Show, who rose from a challenging background to international success.

Recognize your challenges

The Black Dot Philosophy begins with the recognition and acceptance of one's black dots—the personal challenges, obstacles, or difficulties we face in life.

This recognition is a critical first step, as it shifts the individual from denial or avoidance to a position of acknowledgment and readiness to address these issues.

Empowerment through strategy and tactics

The Philosophy emphasizes the power of developing clear strategies and actionable tactics to overcome the black dots. Strategies provide the overarching approach to tackling challenges, while tactics are the specific, practical steps taken to execute these strategies.

Growth and learning
Central to the Black Dot Philosophy is the concept of growth and learning through the process of overcoming challenges. Every black dot presents an opportunity for personal development, increased resilience, and the acquisition of new skills and insights.

Resilience and perseverance
The journey of addressing black dots is inherently tied to the development of resilience and perseverance. Overcoming each challenge builds strength and fortitude, equipping individuals to handle future obstacles more effectively.

The dynamic nature of life's challenges
The Philosophy acknowledges that life's challenges are dynamic and ever-changing. What constitutes a black dot today may evolve or be replaced by new challenges in the future. This understanding fosters adaptability and a continuous commitment to personal growth.

Holistic approach to personal development
The Black Dot Philosophy advocates for a holistic approach to personal development, considering all aspects of one's life, including mental, emotional, physical, and sometimes professional dimensions. This holistic view ensures a balanced and sustainable path to overcoming challenges.

Influence on others and society
Triumphs over individual black dots have a ripple effect, positively influencing others and contributing to societal resilience and progress. These successes serve as inspiration and provide valuable lessons that can benefit the wider community.

Lifelong journey

Lastly, the Philosophy views dealing with black dots as a lifelong journey. It is not about a one-time fix but a continuous process of facing, learning from, and growing through life's challenges. This lifelong journey is characterized by an ongoing process of self-discovery, adaptation, and evolution.

In conclusion, the Black Dot Philosophy is a comprehensive approach to understanding and navigating life's challenges. It transforms the way you can perceive and tackle obstacles, promoting a mindset of growth, resilience, and continuous learning. By embracing this Philosophy, you can turn your black dots into catalysts for personal transformation and success, positively impacting not only your lives but also those around them.

Transformative benefits of conquering your Black Dots

At intervals during this book, you have read about the benefits of overcoming your Black Dots, but here I'd like to pull together all the benefits. You are putting a lot of work into this and so you deserved to be reminded of the payoff of conquering your Black Dots.

It's not just a matter of achieving your goals specifically to overcome the challenges facing you; the Black Dot Philosophy brings a host of broader, usually transformative, benefits.

Personal growth and development

Overcoming black dots often requires developing new skills or enhancing existing ones. Having read this book, for example, how much did you know already about goal-setting, strategy and tactics, let alone mindfulness techniques, the importance of regular self-reflection and the power of discipline and of declarations? This growth is a significant reward in itself.

Increased resilience

Facing and conquering challenges builds resilience. You become more adept at handling adversity in the future.

Improved self-confidence and self-esteem

Successfully overcoming challenges boosts your self-confidence and self-esteem. It reinforces your belief in your capabilities.

There's a profound sense of empowerment that comes from conquering black dots. It's the realization that you have the agency to change your circumstances.

Enhanced problem-solving abilities

Navigating through black dots improves your ability to think strategically and solve problems effectively.

Often, overcoming challenges requires innovative thinking that can be applied to future challenges and opportunities.

Realization of goals and aspirations

Each conquered black dot represents a milestone achieved on the way to your larger goals and aspirations. Overcoming these challenges signifies that you are making tangible progress towards your ultimate vision or life purpose.

Improved mental and emotional well-being

Conquering black dots is likely to alleviate the stress and anxiety associated with those challenges because you may feel more in control of the situation that gave rise to the black dot.

Achieving your goals and overcoming obstacles contributes to a greater sense of happiness and fulfillment.

Positive impact on relationships and social life

Your achievements can serve as an inspiration to others. Overcoming your black dots can motivate those around you to tackle their own challenges.

The journey of overcoming obstacles often involves others, whether for support or collaboration, leading to strengthened relationships.

Professional and career advancement

Overcoming professional challenges can lead to new opportunities, promotions, and career growth.

Successfully tackling difficult projects or situations can enhance your professional reputation and credibility.

Lifestyle improvements

Achieving personal goals, especially those related to health, finances, or personal habits, can significantly improve your overall quality of life.

With each conquered challenge, new doors may open, leading to experiences and opportunities that weren't previously available or apparent.

In conclusion, the rewards and benefits of conquering your Black Dots extend far beyond the immediate resolution of a particular challenge. They contribute to your personal and professional growth, enhance your mental and emotional well-being, improve your relationships, and lead to a more fulfilling and accomplished life. The process transforms not just your ability to tackle obstacles but also shapes your overall character and approach to life.

Real triumphs over Black Dots

Without identifying the individuals by name, these are some examples of real people who have tackled and overcome their Black Dots.

The Entrepreneur who overcame financial hurdles

A young entrepreneur with a vision for a tech startup struggled with financial constraints and lack of industry connections.

Black Dot

The lack of capital and network to launch and grow the business.

Triumph

Through persistent networking, learning, and pitching, the entrepreneur secured funding from angel investors. They also built a strong mentor network that provided invaluable guidance. Their startup eventually gained recognition and success.

The Athlete who defied physical limitations

An athlete faced a severe injury which threatened to end their sports career.

Black Dot

The injury and the possibility of never competing again.

Triumph

Through rigorous physical therapy, mental resilience, and an unwavering commitment to return to the sport, the athlete not only recovered but also came back stronger, eventually winning major competitions and setting new personal records.

The Writer who battled self-doubt

An aspiring writer struggled with self-doubt and fear of rejection which hindered their ability to finish or publish their work.

Black Dot

Paralyzing self-doubt and the challenge of completing and publishing their first novel.

Triumph

The writer joined a supportive writing group, sought feedback from a professional book coach trained to help writers write novels, and dedicated specific times for writing. Overcoming self-doubt, they completed their novel. It was not only published but also received critical acclaim.

The Single Parent who achieved educational goals

A single parent, balancing work and raising children, aspired to complete their college education.

Black Dot

Juggling education with work and parenting responsibilities.

Triumph

Through time management, determination, and support from family and community resources, they attended night classes and online courses, eventually earning their degree, leading to better career opportunities.

The Business Owner who pivoted during a crisis

A small business owner faced the challenge of keeping their business afloat during an economic downturn.

Black Dot

Economic downturn threatening business survival.

Triumph

The owner innovated and adapted their business model, shifting to online platforms and diversifying their product range. This not only saved the business but also expanded their customer base.

These stories exemplify the essence of the Black Dot Philosophy: recognizing challenges, persistently working towards solutions, and ultimately overcoming obstacles. Each narrative highlights the journey of facing and triumphing over a black dot, demonstrating resilience, adaptability, and the power of perseverance.

How the Black Dot Philosophy transforms lives

The Black Dot Philosophy, with its focus on recognizing, confronting, and overcoming personal challenges, has a profound capacity to transform lives. This transformative process leads to significant personal development, a sense of achievement, and often a positive ripple effect in the individual's surroundings

Here are some key ways lives have been transformed through the application of the Black Dot Philosophy:

Enhanced self-awareness

The Philosophy encourages individuals to identify and understand their "black dots," leading to greater self-awareness. This process helps people recognize their strengths and weaknesses, allowing for more targeted personal development.

Development of resilience and grit

Tackling black dots builds resilience. Individuals learn to face adversity, recover from setbacks, and persist despite difficulties.

There's a shift towards a growth mindset, where challenges are seen as opportunities to grow rather than insurmountable obstacles.

Improved problem-solving skills

Confronting and strategizing ways to overcome black dots enhances problem-solving and strategic thinking skills.

People become more adept at finding creative and effective solutions to their problems.

Achievement of personal and professional goals

The Black Dot Philosophy promotes setting clear, achievable goals.

By systematically addressing your Black Dots, you can make significant progress towards, and achieve, your personal and professional aspirations.

Greater emotional well-being

Successfully dealing with Black Dots can lead to reduced stress and anxiety. Achieving goals and overcoming challenges often leads to greater happiness and a sense of fulfillment.

Enhanced relationships and social skills

The process of addressing Black Dots often involves communicating needs and seeking support, enhancing communication skills. Shared experiences in overcoming challenges can lead to deeper, more meaningful relationships.

Positive lifestyle changes

The discipline and focus required to address Black Dots can lead to the development of healthier habits and lifestyle changes. Individuals often achieve a better balance in their personal and professional lives through this transformative process.

Increased confidence and self-efficacy

Each conquered Black Dot boosts confidence and reinforces the belief in one's own capabilities. This increased self-efficacy empowers you to take on new challenges and pursue opportunities you might have previously thought beyond your reach.

Career advancement and opportunities

Overcoming professional Black Dots often leads to career advancement and new opportunities.

The process can expand professional networks, opening doors to new collaborations and ventures.

Inspiration to others

Overcoming Black Dots not only transforms the individual but also serves as inspiration to others enabling the individual to act as a role model.

The journey can positively influence peers, family, and the wider community, encouraging others to confront and overcome their own challenges.

The Black Dot Philosophy acts as a catalyst for profound personal and professional transformation. It empowers individuals to turn challenges into opportunities for growth, leading to improved self-awareness, resilience, problem-solving skills, emotional well-being, and a host of other benefits that extend beyond the individual to positively impact the wider community.

The influence of successfully navigating Black Dot challenges extends far beyond individual achievement. These successes often have a significant and inspiring impact on others, creating a ripple effect of positive change.

How triumphs over Black Dots can influence others

Modeling resilience and perseverance

Successfully overcoming Black Dots serves as a real-life example of resilience and perseverance. Observing someone tackle their challenges head-on can inspire others to face their own difficulties.

It demonstrates that challenges, no matter how daunting, can be overcome with determination and grit, encouraging others to adopt a similar mindset.

Sharing lessons and strategies

Individuals who conquer their Black Dots often share their experiences, strategies, and the lessons they've learned. This knowledge transfer can be invaluable to others facing similar challenges.

Offering insights and guidance based on personal experiences can help others navigate their paths more effectively.

Promoting a growth mindset

Witnessing Black Dot triumphs promotes the concept of a growth mindset—the belief that abilities and intelligence can be developed through dedication and hard work. This shift in mindset can transform how individuals approach their own challenges, fostering a more proactive and positive attitude.

Building supportive communities

Success stories encourage the formation of communities where individuals support each other's growth and development. These communities are often marked by empathy and a deep understanding of shared struggles, creating a nurturing environment for growth.

Enhancing collective well-being

The success of one individual can motivate an entire group, instilling hope and a sense of possibility. Collective well-being, including mental health, is often enhanced when members of a community or group witness and celebrate each other's successes.

Encouraging positive change

When you overcome significant Black Dots, you become a role model for positive change, showing that transformation is possible. You will spur others into action. Your stories can catalyze action in others, spurring them to take steps toward change in their own lives.

Impacting future generations

The legacy of overcoming challenges can impact future generations, instilling values of resilience, perseverance, and adaptability. Success stories provide concrete examples for younger generations to emulate, influencing their approach to life's challenges.

The influence of Black Dot successes on others is profound. These triumphs not only transform the individual but also have the power to inspire, educate, and motivate others. They foster a culture of resilience, growth, and mutual support, contributing to the collective empowerment and well-being of communities and beyond.

Embrace your Black Dot journey

I encourage you to embrace your Black Dot journey with courage, determination, and optimism. Your Black Dots, those challenges and obstacles you face, may feel like barriers now but in reality, they are opportunities for your growth, learning, and personal transformation.

I have given you a vast amount of information to help you navigate your Black Dot journey, so it will be helpful to remind you of what you need to do to start your journey and to see it through to the end.

Recognize and accept your Black Dots

Begin by acknowledging the challenges you face. Understanding and accepting these challenges is the first step in transforming them.

Set clear and achievable goals

Identify what you want to achieve in overcoming these Black Dots. Set goals that are specific, measurable, achievable, relevant, and time-bound.

Develop strategies and tactics

Craft strategies that outline your approach to overcoming these challenges and define specific tactics or actions to execute these strategies. Remember, your tactics should be realistic, consistent, and adaptable.

Seek and offer support

Don't embark on this journey alone. Seek support from friends, family, mentors, or support groups. Similarly, offer support to others on their journeys. Shared experiences can be incredibly empowering.

Embrace a growth mindset

View your Black Dot journey as an opportunity for personal development. Challenges are not insurmountable obstacles but chances to grow stronger, wiser, and more resilient.

Celebrate your progress

Acknowledge and celebrate each victory, no matter how small. These moments of triumph are significant milestones on your journey.

Learn and adapt

Be open to learning from each experience. Adapt your strategies and tactics as you gain new insights and as situations evolve.

Stay committed and persistent

Persistence is key. Stay committed to your goals, even when the journey gets tough. The path to overcoming challenges is rarely linear so be prepared for ups and downs.

Reflect and find meaning

Regularly take time to reflect on your journey. Find meaning in your challenges and the strength you've gained from facing them.

Inspire others

Share your story. Your journey, your struggles, and your triumphs can inspire and motivate others to face their own Black Dots.

Remember, your Black Dot journey is uniquely yours, but the lessons, strengths, and triumphs you gain along the way have the power to influence not just your own life but also those around you.

Embrace this journey with an open heart and mind, and let it shape you into a stronger, more resilient, and more fulfilled individual.

What the collective impact looks like

Individual triumphs over Black Dots leads to a collective impact on our society.

It's not only about your, individual, success. When individuals overcome their challenges, the effects ripple out and influence not just their immediate environment but also the broader fabric of society. The accumulation of these personal victories contributes to building a stronger, more resilient, and progressive society. The story of triumph of one individual inspires resilience in others. These personal victories encourage the formation of support networks and communities that collectively face and overcome challenges.

Each person's journey provides valuable lessons that can benefit others. This sharing of experiences promotes a culture where growth and learning are valued. As people witness real-life examples of growth and adaptation, society begins to shift towards a growth mindset so that challenges begin to be seen as opportunities for development.

An innovative approach that one person develops to overcome a personal Black Dot can go on to inspire creative problem-solving in, say, business or technology or any other field of activity. This culture of innovation and creativity is essential for societal progress and development.

And then there is the element of shared human experience. Recognizing the challenges faced by others fosters empathy and understanding. This recognition strengthens the social fabric by promoting compassion and support. Shared experiences of overcoming obstacles can help break down barriers between different groups within society, fostering unity and cooperation.

The sense of achievement and empowerment gained from overcoming Black Dots contributes to improved mental health, which has a positive impact on overall societal well-being. As more individuals find effective ways to manage and overcome their challenges, there's a collective reduction in stress and anxiety levels in the community.

Triumphs over Black Dots provide role models for future generations, showing them that challenges can be faced and overcome. This legacy of resilience, determination, and success shapes the attitudes and approaches of future generations towards their own challenges.

The skills, insights, and strengths gained from personal journeys can be applied to broader societal issues, driving positive social change. Collective triumphs can influence policies and practices, leading to a more supportive and enabling environment for all members of society.

Each triumph adds to a collective narrative of resilience and possibility, inspiring positive change and shaping a better future for all.

The never-ending journey:
Black Dots as a lifelong endeavor

Dealing with Black Dots is not a one-time task. Change is a constant in our lives and so while you are engaged in the process of monitoring and adapting your approach to your Black Dots, others may be forming and will need to be dealt with. It is a continuous and evolving process throughout life.

This is realistic and deeply empowering. Facing and overcoming challenges is a continuous part of life but you have already shown, by reaching the end of this book, that you are strong enough to face your own challenges. You will gain in strength as you make your plans and follow through on action to deal with your Black Dots. The journey itself is what will foster your personal growth, resilience, wisdom, and enable you to gain a deeper understanding of yourself, those around you and of life.

Let me remind you what you gain from embracing the Black Dot Philosophy.

Continuous growth and development

The journey of addressing and overcoming Black Dots is ongoing. As we grow and evolve, so do our challenges.

Each Black Dot we encounter and navigate shapes us, contributing to our personal growth and evolution.

Changing nature of challenges

Black Dots evolve. They change over time. What seems daunting today may be a stepping stone for future challenges. Each new challenge presents an opportunity for learning something new about ourselves and the world around us.

Lifelong resilience

A lifelong journey with Black Dots builds our resilience and adaptability. This resilience becomes a fundamental part of our character, helping us to face future challenges with greater ease and confidence.

Perspective and wisdom

Over time, dealing with various challenges provides deeper insights into life and our responses to it. We gain wisdom not just about how to overcome obstacles but also about what truly matters to us. This journey instills in us a more mature perspective on life's ups and downs. We learn to see challenges as natural and integral parts of our journey.

Inspiration to others

A lifelong commitment to facing and overcoming Black Dots serves as an inspiration to others. It shows that while life is not without challenges, continuous effort can lead to meaningful progress and fulfillment. Applying the Black Dot Philosophy leaves a legacy of perseverance, resilience, and the ability to adapt and grow, which can inspire current and future generations.

Embracing Life's complexity

The never-ending journey with Black Dots teaches us to accept and embrace the uncertainty and complexity of life. It encourages us to find joy and fulfillment in the journey itself, not just the destination.

Continuous self-discovery

Each challenge provides an opportunity for self-discovery. We continually learn more about our strengths, weaknesses, desires, and fears. This self-knowledge enables us to live more authentically and make choices that are aligned with our true selves.

Think about your own Black Dot journey

I have summarized the core principles of the Black Dot Philosophy, and demonstrated its transformational potential and the enduring impact it will have on your life.

To help you embed the Philosophy into your outlook, I suggest you do this.

- Summarize the key principles of the Black Dot Philosophy in your own words
- Reflect on how the Black Dot Philosophy has transformed your life or perspective
- Write a personal reflection on your Black Dot journey
- Describe the specific rewards and benefits you've experienced
- Express your gratitude for the insights and changes it has brought to your life
- Share any personal insights or lessons learned during your Black Dot journey
- Share how your Black Dot successes have influenced those around you
- Consider how you plan to apply the Black Dot Philosophy in your future endeavors
- Share your vision for the future and how the Black Dot Philosophy will continue to be a part of it.

SOME FINAL THOUGHTS...

To all those who embark on the journey of understanding by applying the Black Dot Philosophy

Your life is a canvas of endless possibilities. Every challenge, every black dot you face, is not just an obstacle, but a stepping stone towards greater strength, deeper understanding, and more profound fulfillment.

Embrace these challenges as opportunities to grow, to learn, and to transform.

You are strong

You possess an incredible capacity for resilience and adaptation. Within you lies the power to overcome, to evolve, and to emerge stronger from each challenge you face. Remember, the Black Dots do not define you; your response to them does. Your journey through these challenges is a testament to your strength, your will, and your potential.

Now that you have read the Black Dot Philosophy, I encourage you to see it not just as a book but as a mirror to reflect on your own life. See in it the parallels to your challenges and the potential for your growth. Identify your own Black Dots. Acknowledge them, understand them, and strategize ways to address them. Take small, consistent steps.

Remember, progress is incremental. As you journey through your Black Dots, share your experiences and lessons with others. Your story can be a source of inspiration and encouragement for many.

This is a continuous journey. You will achieve your goals but there is no final destination, only the path of growth, learning, and transformation as you adapt and deal with successive Black Dots.

Be an agent of change. Embody the principles of the Black Dot Philosophy in your daily life. Your actions, your resilience, and your triumphs can ripple outwards, creating a positive impact far beyond your own life.

The journey to overcome your Black Dots is not just about overcoming challenges; it's about unlocking your true potential, discovering your strengths, and making a meaningful impact. Embrace this journey with an open heart and a committed spirit. The path may not always be easy, but the growth, the learning, and the fulfillment you will find along the way will be immeasurably rewarding.

Thank you for your attention and engagement with this book. Let's embark on this journey together, with courage, determination, and the unwavering belief in our ability to transform challenges into opportunities for growth.

FOLLOW UP QUESTIONS

The following ten questions are for those who have gone through the process of identifying, strategizing, and overcoming their Black Dot challenges

1. What was the most significant Black Dot challenge you faced, and how did you approach it differently this time?
2. Can you share a specific tactic or strategy that made a significant impact in achieving one of your Black Dot goals?
3. How did the concept of Black Dots change your perspective on setting and achieving goals?
4. Were there any unexpected insights or realizations that emerged during your journey with the Black Dot concept?
5. In what ways has overcoming your Black Dots influenced your overall well-being and quality of life?
6. Can you recall a moment when you felt particularly empowered by the progress you made in tackling a Black Dot?
7. How have you applied the strategies and tactics you learned to new challenges or goals in your life?
8. Has the Black Dot concept influenced your ability to adapt to unexpected setbacks or obstacles?
9. What advice would you give to others who are looking to use the Black Dot approach to achieve their goals?
10. Looking back, how has the concept of Black Dots shaped your personal growth and self-awareness?

These questions can provide valuable insights into how individuals have utilized the Black Dot concept to navigate their challenges and achieve their goals.

THE BLACK DOT RESOURCE LIBRARY

The following are a variety of resources, websites, articles, apps, books, and templates, some of which I alluded to in the book. I thought it would be beneficial to compile a resource directory so you can tap into this vast pool of support, if you want, as you work through the book, the workbook, and your individual action plans.

The single most important resource you should take a look at is www.mindtools.com.

Mind Tools is a website for personal and professional development. The site includes articles, tools, podcasts, and videos covering various topics such as leadership, strategy, problem-solving, and productivity. They focus on providing practical advice and techniques to improve skills in these areas. I've listed a few of the resources in the following pages.

This is an alphabetical list by topic.

Accountability

» StickK is a commitment platform for personal accountability. Visit stickk.com.

Beliefs

» *The Believing Brain: From Ghosts and Gods to Politics and Conspiracies* by Michael Shermer.
» *Understanding and Challenging Your Beliefs*, an article on mindtools.com.

Big Five Personality Traits

» You can take an online Big Five personality assessment *Understand Myself* at understandmyself.com.
» And you could read, *Personality: What Makes You the Way You Are* by Daniel Nettle.

Discipline

» Track your goals and ensure discipline by using *Beeminder* at beeminder.com.
» Brian Tracy's book, *No Excuses! The Power of Self-Discipline* gives more on the topic.

Eisenhower Matrix (task prioritization)

The "Eisenhower Matrix," also known as the "Urgent-Important Matrix," is a time management tool that helps prioritize tasks by urgency and importance. It's named after Dwight D. Eisenhower, who was known for his incredible ability to sustain productivity.

Eisenhower himself did not create the matrix as we know it today. The book by Stephen Covey, *The 7 Habits of Highly Effective People*, popularized the concept attributing the basic idea of the matrix to Eisenhower's decision-making process.

» Read the article *Eisenhower's Urgent/Important Principle* on mindtools.com.

Guided Meditations

» headspace.com offers a range of guided meditations.
» The book *Wherever You Go* by Jon Kabat-Zinn is an exploration of mindfulness meditation.

Habits

» Have fun with a gamified habit-building app called *Habitica* at habitica.com.

» The book by James Clear, *Atomic Habits*, is a comprehensive guide on habit formation and a must read.

Myer Briggs (personality assessment)

» You can find the official Myer Briggs Type Indicator test at MBTI's website, mbtionline.com.

» The co-creator of the test, Isabel Briggs Myer, wrote a book about it. *Gifts Differing: Understanding Personality Type*.

Journaling

» These resources cover a range of journaling styles and preferences. Find one that suits you.

» The classic book by Julia Cameron, *The Artist's Way*, promotes daily journaling for creativity.

Free and Paid Apps

» *Day One* is a personal journaling app offering daily prompts, customizable templates, and features such as tracking time, date, weather, and moon phase. It's suitable for those preferring a freeform digital diary style. Available on iOS and Android, Day One has a free version and a premium subscription, currently at $3/month.

» *5 Minute Journal* by Intelligent Change LLC provides a guided gratitude journaling format with morning and evening prompts for reflection. It aims to make journaling a quick, daily habit and is available on iOS and Android. The app is currently free, with a $4.99/month subscription for additional features.

» *Daylio* is ideal for quick, mood-based journaling. It allows you to track daily activities and moods without extensive writing. It's great for setting and tracking personal goals and habits. Daylio is currently free with a $2.99/month subscription for premium features and is available on both iOS and Android.

» *Momento* is a versatile journaling app that can be used for various purposes like personal or work journaling. It connects with your social networks to import activities and offers a "This Day" feature for reminiscing. Momento is currently free with a $2.49/month subscription for extra features, available only on iOS.

» *DailyBean* offers a simple and almost game-like approach to journaling. You can track your day using mood beans and add details about your emotions, social activities, sleep, etc. DailyBean is available on both iOS and Android platforms.

Mindfulness

» A mindfulness and meditation app is Calm, at calm.com.
» The classic book is *The Miracle of Mindfulness* by Thich Nhat Hanh.

Organization

» Try Evernote for note-taking and organization: evernote.com.
» An app at todoist.com includes features for task categorization.
» And for the life-changing experience of getting your house (literally) in order, read *The Life-Changing Magic of Tidying Up* by Marie Kondo. It is, for the present, *the* guide to organizing and decluttering.

Overcoming Setbacks

» *Failing Forward: Turning Mistakes into Stepping Stones for Success* by John C. Maxwell.

» *Adversity Quotient: Turning Obstacles into Opportunities* by Paul G. Stoltz.
» *Trust Yourself* by Melody Wilding
» You can find a piece on *7 Ways to Bounce Back from Setbacks* in *Psychology Today*, free, online.

Purpose

» A popular philosophical exploration of life's purpose can be found in *Man's Search for Meaning* by Viktor Frankl.
» *Why Bother? Discover the Desire for What's Next* by Jen Louden is a guide to finding your profound purpose.
» Type *Seven Ways to Find Your Purpose in Life* into your browser to find that article from the Greater Good Magazine.
» There is more on aligning with your purpose and finding motivation at Section 4 of *Inflection: a Roadmap for Leaders at a Crossroads* by Sharath Jeevan, OBE.

SMART (Specific, Measurable, Achievable, Relevant, Time-bound goals)

The term "SMART" in the context of goal-setting stands for Specific, Measurable, Achievable, Relevant, and Time-bound. This acronym is used to guide the setting of objectives, making them clear and reachable.

The origin of the SMART goals concept is often attributed to a paper written by George T. Doran, published in 1981 titled "There's a S.M.A.R.T. way to write management's goals and objectives." It appeared in the November issue of Management Review. Doran's paper is cited as the first prominent usage of the term in the context of goal-setting.

Although the SMART acronym is widely referenced in management and personal development literature, it's not originally from a book specifically titled "SMART" or "SMART Goals." Instead, it has been elaborated upon in various books and articles about management, productivity, and personal development following Doran's initial introduction of the concept.

For an in-depth look at setting SMART goals, refer to the article *How to Set SMART Goals* on the website *MindTools* at www.mindtools.com. It offers valuable insights into creating effective and measurable objectives.

The book by Charles Duhigg, *Smarter Faster Better: The Secrets of Being Productive* explains how we can get better at the things we do. It shows how productivity relies on making certain choices in our daily decisions or our big ambitions. The choices we make separate the merely busy from the genuinely productive.

Spreadsheets for Tracking

» *Google Sheets*, at sheets.google.com, is a versatile and collaborative spreadsheet tool.
» There are a wide variety of templates online for tracking your goals; use *templates for goal tracking* as your search term in your browser of choice.

SWOT Analysis

SWOT stands for Strengths, Weaknesses, Opportunities, and Threats, and so a SWOT analysis is a technique for assessing these four aspects of any response to a current-state situation, whether in your personal life, or your professional or business life.

SWOT Analysis is a tool that can help you to analyze what your company does best now, and to devise a successful strategy for the future. SWOT can also uncover areas that are holding you back, or that—in a business context—your competitors could exploit if you don't protect yourself.

A SWOT analysis examines both internal and external factors—that is, what's going on inside and outside you, or your organization.

So, some of these factors will be within your control and some will not. In either case, the wisest action you can take in response will become clearer once you've discovered, recorded, and analyzed as many factors as you can.

Read the article *SWOT Analysis: Understanding Your Business, Informing Your Strategy* on mindtools.com.

Task Management and Calendaring

» Google Calendar integrates calendar and task management (calendar.google.com.)

The Life Wheel (life balance assessment)

» You can find the *Life Wheel Template* on various coaching websites, including mindtools.com.
» Mindtools.com also has a detailed guide on using the Life Wheel called *Life Wheel Explanation.*

Timeline

A text-based timeline document is a great way to keep track of deadlines and ensure progress on your projects. Here's a simple template you can use either in a text document such as Word, or in a spreadsheet, which makes for easier tracking and updating. Adjust the dates, tasks, and milestones to fit your specific needs.

[Your Project Name]: Timeline and Deadlines
Start Date: [Start Date]
Week 1: [Date Range]

• Task 1: [Description]
• Milestone: [Description of a key achievement or checkpoint]

Week 2: [Date Range]

- Task 2: [Description]
- Milestone: [Description]

Week 3: [Date Range]

- Task 3: [Description]
- [Any additional notes or checkpoints]

Mid-Project Review: [Date]

- Review progress
- Adjust upcoming tasks and dates as needed

Week 4: [Date Range]

- Task 4: [Description]
- Milestone: [Description]

Week 5: [Date Range]

- Task 5: [Description]
- [Any additional notes or checkpoints]

Final Stages: [Date Range]

- Finalize Project
- Review all completed tasks
- Final Milestone: [Completion of the project or a significant achievement]

Project Completion Date: [End Date]

- Final review and wrap-up
- Celebrate the completion!

This timeline is a guideline and can be adjusted as needed. Regularly reviewing and updating your timeline will help keep you on track.

Time Management

» Track your time spent on applications and websites with rescuetime.com.
» Read *Getting Things Done: The Art of Stress-Free Productivity* by David Allen.

Vision

» *The Vision Driven Leader* by Michael Hyatt has insights on creating and realizing a powerful vision.

Vision Boards

A vision board is a tool used for visualization and goal-setting where the board serves as a visual representation of one's goals and aspirations. The concept is based on the law of attraction, which suggests that focusing on positive or negative thoughts brings positive or negative experiences into a person's life.

The process involves creating a physical or digital board where you place images, words, and symbols that represent what you want to achieve. This could be in any area of life: career, relationships, health,

personal growth, etc. By placing the board somewhere you will see it often, the idea is that you regularly reinforce these goals and desires, helping to focus your thoughts and actions towards achieving them.

Here is an example of a vision board used as an inspiration and daily reminder of a person's aspirations. It features various images and words that represent different life goals, such as healthy living, travel, success, happiness, financial freedom, strong relationships, and personal growth.

» Check out the app at visuapp.co that's a digital platform for creating vision boards.

Unlock Your Full Potential with
The Black Dot Philosophy

Congratulations on beginning your journey with *The Black Dot Philosophy*. The insights you've gained are just the first step towards lasting transformation. To continue your path to personal and professional growth, we invite you to explore the full suite of resources we offer:

- **Skill-Building Workshops**: Tailored programs for organizations and companies seeking to empower their teams through practical, hands-on training in resilience and growth mindset strategies.
- **The Companion Workbook**: A hands-on guide designed to deepen your understanding of the book's teachings, with exercises and reflections for personal development.
- **Personalized Coaching**: One-on-one sessions that provide focused guidance, helping you to apply The Black Dot Philosophy to your unique life circumstances.
- **Speaking Engagements**: Inspirational talks that bring the powerful lessons of The Black Dot Philosophy to your events and gatherings.

To learn more about these opportunities and to join our growing community, visit www.theblackdotphilosophy.com and sign up for exclusive updates, resources, and more.

As a token of our appreciation for your commitment to growth, visit **www.theblackdotphilosophy.com** to receive a special resource to complement your journey with The Black Dot Philosophy.

GRATITUDE

There are several people to whom I owe my deepest gratitude for their support and contributions to this book:

To Mike Kroplin: You were an amazing mentor and leader. Your simple drawing of a black circle sparked an idea and ultimately a philosophy that has transformed countless lives.

To Carla Green: The owner of Clarity Designworks, you did an amazing job designing the front and back book covers along with the interior design. You also walked me through the publishing process from start to finish. You were an invaluable resource.

To Ruth Bullivant: An experienced writer, editor, and book coach, you took my manuscript filled with great content and, through your incredible patience and expertise, turned it into a truly great book.

To Miguel Lopes: You were my go-to person for all my technical needs and much more. Without your support and knowledge, it would have been virtually impossible to have a Portuguese version of the book along with a Portuguese version of the www.blackdotphilosophy.com

To Melanie Herschorn: The owner of VIP Book Marketing, you have been instrumental in the development and implementation of the marketing of my book. You are an amazing resource and incredibly talented and knowledgeable.

Thank you all for being the guiding lights in my journey.

ABOUT THE AUTHOR

Jerry Mark Fish, Chartered Leadership Fellow and founder of The Black Dot Philosophy, Inc., established in January 2024, is a beacon of resilience and transformation. His company offers elite coaching and speaking services worldwide, bringing to life the process expounded by his insightful book and workbook (available in both paper and digital versions). Discover more at www.theblackdotphilosophy.com.

Jerry had an illustrious career that spanned nearly four decades in the financial services industry. His path was marked by rapid ascension through top sales and management professional roles to recruitment, in 1993, into a leadership role at New York Life Insurance Company. Beginning in the San Francisco General Office, he swiftly advanced and, at the same time, significantly enhanced the company's growth and market share in the four different agencies he led as their Managing Partner. In 2016, he was promoted to Pacific Zone Vice President, where he was responsible for growth and market share in the Western United States until his retirement in 2018.

A Chartered Leadership Fellow since 2010, Jerry divides his time between Lisbon, Portugal, and San Diego, California. He has one son, Tyler, who is a successful technology professional in San Diego. Jerry's passions include golf, travel, reading, and writing. He is the author of two screenplays, *Veterans Day* and *Founders*, and looks forward to continuing his creative endeavors.

Jerry's life is a testament to the human spirit's capacity to endure, evolve, and excel amid life's myriad challenges. Through *The Black Dot Philosophy*, he imparts this wisdom, inspiring others to transform their adversities into opportunities for personal and professional growth.

www.ingramcontent.com/pod-product-compliance
Lightning Source LLC
Chambersburg PA
CBHW071147130626
46553CB00004B/1562